HITCH-HIKING TO GOD

Wm. D. Leaf

Dedication

The list of those who God used to impact my life and helped me is too long to list. God knows who each of you are and what place you had in the areas of my life. Special thanks are of course directed to the spiritual family who allowed me to stay in their home and learn about the things of the Lord.

Special thanks goes to my wife Nancy who spent much time encouraging me and performing the technical details that comes with putting together   manuscripts.

To Fay, who spent countless hours in front of her computer doing the editing and changing of sentences and word meanings in order to present a more balanced and perfect picture on certain words and their meanings.

To Vera and Shells, who were more than willing to offer my wife and I support whenever needed.

Also to Jen wherever she is, the Lord used you to hold me accountable to writing from the real me and not behind some hidden wall. Had it not been for you, perhaps my true writing abilities would never have come to be known.

Wm. D. Leaf

Introduction

God still is in control and works within the lives of people today. We all have a testimony to share. My life and the involvement the Lord showed towards me are nothing short of a miracle. I am very much mindful of this fact. He did not have to do for me the things He did but to God be the glory for doing so.

The value of a solitary life coming under the hand of a loving God and undergoing change is more precious than gold or silver. However, I must caution the reader, change did not come easily for me and I pushed God to the limit in some of the things I did as His child. Yet Praise God, I survived under His care. To this day I shudder to think of where I would be had God given up on me. As you, the reader, read this story, at times it will shock you as to my insanity and barefaced defiance before the Lord. However, hang in there and finish the story for there is a happy ending

Summary

L ife on a farm was what gave me many hours of happiness as a child, but there were many hours of sadness as well. Upon leaving the farm and going out on my own, my life took many different directions of survival; the basics of life being one of these. Even though it will seem in the beginning that I never could get out of what I had placed myself into, you will read how the God who created all had the power to create in me a new heart and make me a person who was able to function in a way pleasing to Him. I know there will be many who want to ask questions of me, I welcome all correspondence and I promise to answer each letter personally and with my fullest attention.

Thank you,
Wm. D. Leaf
P.O. Box 553
Coos Bay, Oregon 97420
hitchhiking_to_god@hotmail.com

Table of Contents

Chapter One

A Perfect Fit

"Now therefore ye are no more strangers and for-
eigners, but fellow citizens with the saints; and
of the household of God; And are built upon the
foundation of the apostles and prophets, Jesus
Christ himself being the chief corner stone. In
whom all the building fitly framed together
groweth unto a holy temple in the Lord: In whom
ye also are builded together for an habitation of
God through the Spirit." (Ephesians 2:19-22)

I have to admit that I struggled a great deal with a feeling
that I did not fit in the body of Christ or belong there for
that matter. Even though I knew I was saved, a strong
sense of inadequacy as to who I was greatly dominated my
walk. Owing to this shadow hanging over me I obviously
withdrew from others. Even though I lived among fellow
believers, yet the inside person and the outside person were
two separate individuals.

The Lord had his work cut out for Him in this area of
my life because of this constant struggle. It took many

communications back and forth between us to convince me that I was a child of God and that I belonged in the body of Christ. Satan, of course, was having a hay-day over this weakness within me of feeling that I did not belong. He was very cruel and unrelenting in his attacks to keep me from entering my position in Christ. To make matters worse, I actually believed the lies he told me. There was no doubt that I suffered from an identity crisis which needed to be corrected big time.

Even while in the world I had no clear understanding of who I was. I spent years aimlessly going from one thing to another, like a bee who goes from flower to flower collecting pollen. Soon, I had collected enough samples of what the world had to offer while busy looking for meaning and direction and I became stuck in my own world of quicksand and hopelessness.

Owing to formed and set patterns of sin within me I was greatly crippled in my ability to function in the same way as those around me who seemed so happy and joyful. I had scar tissue from inner wounds that had never healed. There were things that I endured in my early life as a child. There was "baggage" that I had picked up and carried while living on the streets. All of these played a combined role in my condition as a new-born member of the body of Christ.

I was truly saved, and I praise God for that. Yet, due to a previous dysfunctional life I was not a whole person. I spilled into the new life wrecked and dislocated with fragments and pieces scattered about from one end of my universe to the other.

My life in Christ underwent a series of constant fine tunings and adjustments brought on by the Holy Spirit working within me. The perfecting, upgrading, renewing and recreating into the image of Jesus and preparation for a future work and ministry seemed a million miles away from reality so much of the time.

Too often we labor as God's child under a heavy load of disgrace and awkwardness over some past event. This continues to hold us confined to its mooring due to scar tissue that has never been removed, but remains just out of sight of conscious memory.

In order to get on with life and be a survivor we learn to stuff, bury and cover up those things that have caused us pain and shame. However, if those things continue to remain inside us, lurking just below the surface areas of our lives, then those very things will slowly begin to form, bend, shape, and even control us at times.

The good news is that the Lord's grace not only saves us from sin, but His grace also extends as a healing stream directed to those who are undone and broken. His workings within us go way beyond that which man can do on our behalf. He reaches areas in our lives that are far beyond what we can ever personally visualize or expect to achieve.

As God's children we should not bury our wounds one on top of the other, but rather we need to bring them to the Lord so that He can heal them one by one. The healing process is not always easy and at times will also require certain steps to be taken by us. It is sometimes easier to remain in the shadows before the Lord, instead of living up to the demands that healing places upon us in order for us to be made whole.

Are we willing to be obedient and trusting or do we hide under a hardness of heart? Do we hold unyielding to our yesterdays, for in them we have established well-known and time honored safety zones? These have become the prominent foundations for our justification in how we act towards others and how we abide under this world's code of honor. From this position we rule, reign and establish our empire over the heads of all others, without any thought of repentance over damage to others caused by our actions.

In addition to our attempts at covering and stuffing we

take on the role of acting out false appearances of happiness and well being. This type of 'image playing' divides us into a man of many faces or masks. One appearance establishes us as being in control and well adjusted, whereas the inner man is hurting and censored.

We flip-flop through life out of harmony with the inner and outer compartments of our total blueprint. We are conditioned to always display an "I'm ok," pre-recorded comeback to any and all who would take the time to make inquiries of our well-being. We see those on the street and in passing we fall into standard greetings that are so common and ritualistic in everyday conversation, yet accepted as normal and polite in our culture today. People expect this from us in everyday greetings and we also expect that from others. It is no surprise then that in a huge populated city a person can be just as alone as if he or she were on the moon. We have become strangers in a strange land and no-one dares shatter the mood for fear that he or she is looked down upon as being out of whack or strange.

Even as a kid growing up on a farm I learned the benefit of mask-wearing at an early age. Of course, I did not do a good job of it, for a person who does not have a foundation from which to operate can only sink as time and seasons wash against the framework of the soul.

However, none of the above problems or the condition I grew up in was above the Lord's power to heal me. He worked with me and together we tackled my lack of confidence and feelings of inadequacy. He did this in one way by bringing truth to my soul and imparting knowledge of His love to me. I will never forget what took place on one particular day.

I was working at a fast-food restaurant as a janitor. While on the job I was cleaning the bathroom. There in the corner of the wash basin was a small puddle of water in which a "fly" was stranded and appeared ready to die. My attention was drawn to this situation and I stopped doing my cleaning and instead I focused on the situation. Strangely enough I had a compassion for this fly and it moved me to want to rescue him from his dire straits. I placed the fly on a paper towel in the sunshine that came through the window above. From there I watched the fly go through the recovery progress, which was done so in steps. It did not take long and before I knew it he had totally recovered and flew away to live another day.

The Lord then spoke to me in this way, "My son you were as that fly, you were ready to die. You were sin covered and helpless to save yourself. In a similar way to that fly you were not wanted and no-one cared. Yet, I had compassion for you as you did for that fly. I reached down my hand and set you in the sunshine of my love and restored you back to health. When no-one else cared whether you lived or died, I showed you compassion and I delivered you."

That was one way of many that the Lord communicated His love to me and showed me my place within His kingdom as a child rightfully belonging in the body. I wish I could say that from that conversation I was no longer disturbed by oppressive thoughts, but this was not the case. However, over the coming months I continued to digest more of His word and as a result I soon got beyond this particular problem that bothered me.

Chapter 2 of the book of Ephesians and the part of "fitting in" were the very verses that the Lord used to help me recapture my footing as to who I was in Him and how He saw me as His child. I cannot begin to count the times I had to keep repeating these words over and over again. "I am saved, I have a right to be here, and I belong." Love, acceptance and forgiveness were the key in those days of my early Christian beginnings. My individual "fly condition" and the body of Christ within the local assembly were my biggest worlds at that time. I needed healing and I needed change and transformation.

Chapter Two

A Horrible Pit

"He brought me up also out of a horrible pit, out of the miry clay, and set my feet upon a rock, and established my goings. And he hath put a new song in my mouth, even praise unto our God: many shall see it, and fear, and shall trust in the Lord." (Psalms 40:2-3)

I have found this section of God's word to be so appropriate in the way it describes me as to the condition I was in and the goodness of God presented towards me. Therefore, I divided up the verse into sections and from there will tell my story as best as I can with the Lord's help. The word phrase, "horrible pit" is perfect to launch into what my life was like in those days.

I did not grow up in a secure, non-strife, non-divorce family environment. After my dad and mom divorced I ended up in an orphanage for a season and it was there that I got my first hand encounter of abusive violence and mistreatment. I was around two or three years old at the time. I was the youngest of three brothers and we also had a younger sister, but she never made it to the orphanage due to her infant age, it was just my two brothers and I. Our mom abandoned us and Dad had no choice other than to have us placed in the orphanage. That was how my life began. From this "horrible pit" I began digging and enlarging it from within, never once realizing what I was doing.

Finally the day came for us to be discharged from the orphanage; I was still very young and did not really know what was going on. However, I do remember being in the back seat of my Dad's car and having a strange woman sitting next to him. I don't recall doing much talking; the whole car ride was mostly carried forth in stillness. I was told she was my new mom (whatever that meant) and that we boys were now starting a new life. My eldest brother did not seem too pleased over this new mom thing, but I sure was happy to be leaving. To this day I wonder if my Dad knew what kind of things happened to me during my stay at the orphanage. My eldest brother knew, but he would never say what it was, obviously whatever it was it must have been bad.

The year was somewhere around 1955 or 1956. Dad moved us out into the country to an old farmhouse with 50 acres of land. There was so much room to move around and run after grasshoppers and gophers! We had chickens, pigs, (the pigs never saw fit to stay in their pens) cows and turkeys and later pigeons too. For a child this farm was the greatest place to live, I don't regret the life I lived as far as the country was concerned, yet all of that seclusion was fleeting for soon trouble erupted between my eldest brother and our step mom. To make it simple, they just did not get along.

I too had my own problems to contend with and Mary, (my step mom) was now becoming my worst nightmare. Just because I moved out of the orphanage did not mean my personal problems stayed behind, but unfortunately I brought my "bedwetting" problem to this new bed. Sure this was embarrassing to me but even worse than that were the beatings I got each and every morning, like clockwork on the hour. When I awoke in the mornings and realized I had wet the bed again it paralysed me with a crippling fear. Sure enough, Mary would walk into the room and stand there at the foot of the bed and say nothing, but just stare at me with no expression on her face. Her belt hung down at her side, hovering and intimidating. Let me tell you that belt was the biggest one I ever laid eyes on! After what seemed like an eternity of eye-to-eye contact her next move was also unsurprising as well. She went into a mode of total frenzy. She grabbed the covers from off the bed and they went flying helter-skelter and I with them and that was stage two. The grand finale stage, (which I got to play a role in) was that I was given the singing part by screaming and crying as the belt flew at me like a cyclone in a closet. Oh what fun we had! The next day the whole party began again and this went on for month after month. To this day I wonder why Dad and my brothers sat out in the front room and did nothing, but remain silent during those times. Whatever Dad thought of this tactic imposed on me by Mary is not known to me, He was not "big" on talking about such things, nor did He ever support me over injustice; that was just the way Dad did things. One day, after another conventional routine and things in the house went back to normal; (whatever that was) I asked Mary how I could stop wetting the bed. Why I didn't ask her this sooner is beyond me, but I shall never forget her reply. Without a moments hesitation she said, "Pray about it." Three little words yet those words of instruction were soon to be the most important words in my little life. This particular event took place during the first summer we arrived on the farm and that very night before going to bed I said my very first uncomplicated childlike prayer. So that very night I climbed into bed and as I lay there I said; "Please God don't let me wet the bed tonight." That is all there was to it, nothing deep and theological, but rather short, simple and real. I was desperate; that much was certain. If I ever needed help over this problem it was then.

The very next thing I knew it was morning and when I awoke my sheets were dry and I was in good shape. I shall never forget the joy I felt in me that morning; I literally flew out of bed and ran into the living room to announce the good news. I do recall upon telling them what had happened, their level of gladness was a big zero. I was so thrilled, yet they, (my step mom and brothers) acted like it was not a big thing. As for me, this was the ultimate miracle of miracles.

Not only did God help me in a personal way, but He also delivered me out of the hand of my step mom's belt. It was like a double blessing in one. However, a much greater work was done in my heart that day. I knew from that moment on that a mighty powerful thing had happened in which there was no explanation other than a "God thing." That morning when I awoke and instantly realized my situation, something inside of me was changed from that time on. I inherited knowledge of God which in turn released within me a new kind of understanding of the spiritual things in life. From then on I knew God existed and I defended Him and the Bible even though I had no idea who or what God was, neither had I ever read the Bible before. Yet I knew He was real. From that day on I never wet the bed again and every night before going to sleep I said my prayers. I now had a source of security which I called on many times in the future. Without Him in my life, providing protection from things that I later on engaged in, without Him answering future prayers of mine when I was in serious situations, some even life-threatening, I would not be here today.

"Ye have not chosen me, but I have chosen you, and ordained you, that ye should go and bring forth fruit, and that your fruit should remain: that whatsoever ye shall ask of the Father in my name, he may give it you." (John 15:16)

The mystery of the ages within my heart is, "Why me God? What has moved you to place your hand upon me and put your Spirit upon my life? Did you see something in me that day long ago when I prayed concerning my bedwetting that put me on your favorite list? Or was it before I was born that you decided to hand pick me from among the multitudes to enter into your program of care and improvement? What was in me that could have caused you to give attention to a person such as me? When did I inherit your compassion upon my life? Was it brought on by something I did or said sometime or was it brought on by a predetermined appointment given to me at birth? Perhaps Lord I might never know until I enter heaven's gate. But for now Lord I am content to accept your love and be thankful that you have chosen me from out of weak conditions and given me life." Not only was there open hostility concerning my eldest brother, as I mentioned earlier, but Dad and Mary were having serious marriage problems too, which rapidly escalated from bad to worse before my very eyes. This marriage did not end fast but it died a slow death. It would have been better for all of us if it had died quickly, but Dad for some reason tried to maintain it, and I can only guess he did so for us boys. However, in the end the marriage played itself out in the most bizarre ways and once again my horrible pit got dug a little bit deeper and wider.

Mary was not mentally sick as we think of mental illness today. However, she did have a deep-rooted problem of some kind and this made her very unpredictable in her emotions. One moment she was ok the next moment she was yelling and tossing things around. Many times Dad spent hours in the bedroom or the next room trying to calm her down after some "blow up" over a word said or a look given. I remember at times it was so tense in the home that my eldest brother and Dad took the guns out of the house for Mary could not be trusted to not use them against us.

Mary also had a religious side to her as well. She would drag us kids off to church and made us three brothers suffer a two-hour excursion on our Sunday mornings listening to a Sunday school teacher and a dry sermon. Dad never went, but he allowed Mary to take us in her 53 Chevy. The only thing I ever learned from my brief church attendance was that the first four books of the New Testament were Matthew, Mark, Luke and John.

The marriage finally ended with a closing grand slam event, I think I was in the fourth or fifth grade at the time. Both of my two older brothers were out of the home during this time, it was just dad, Mary and I. Mary brought legal charges against Dad and through the nature of these charges she managed to have him brought before a judge with testimonies from her friends which built support on her behalf to whatever things she claimed concerning our Dad and his mental problems. The end result was that Dad was committed to a mental hospital at the state for observation.

This turn of events placed me in an unsafe environment for I now was alone with Mary at the farm. She paced back and forth through the house knowing sooner or later Dad would get out of lock down and would return. I knew that too, and it was beyond my twelve- year-old mind to comprehend what would happen when that day arrived, I soon was to find out.

It was spring and life on the farm was recovering from the previous winter. Mary had her brother come out that day and use my Dad's tractor to plough up the garden spot in order to get ready for the early planting. Word had reached us that Dad had been discharged from the mental ward. Upon receiving this information Mary became uneasy, knowing Dad was out there somewhere yet not knowing when, where or how he would strike, (we both knew he would, it was just a matter of time) this only added more tension to an already explosive environment. I wish I had not been there, but my horrible pit only kept getting deeper with each new shovel full of dirt. Even in this the Lord's hand was upon me, not by removing me out of my troubles, but upon me during these "digging times," when I would have rather been somewhere else instead.

That day came and went like the others however, when the sun went down day turned into night and Dad appeared at the house. It was around nine or so that evening, Mary and I both saw Dad's car pull into the driveway. Mary's brother, John, had long since gone home for the evening, had he been there things would have been much different for his presence there with Mary would have pushed my Dad's abilities to control his anger way over the edge for John and Dad did not get along anyway.

Dad was a man with much pride in his heart and this thing concerning being in a mental hospital was by far the biggest attack on his pride and reputation for a man such as him. I feared Dad's anger and I knew what Dad was like, for I had had his anger directed at me on more than one occasion. I knew what it was like to have him hit me square in the head so hard that I was knocked down and left lying in the place where I landed knocked out and hurt. However, on this day his past anger was nothing in contrast to what I now witnessed.

Dad had apparently spent the day in the tavern drinking and getting madder by the moment. When he arrived that night he was drunk and was in no mood for telling jokes. Mary upon seeing his drunken state instantly started nagging him and it was not long before nagging turned into yelling and yelling escalated to shoving, followed by hitting and screaming. I was in the bedroom in fear like never before. Dad had come out that night to kill her and him too. To this day I don't know where I stood in this, but most likely he would have killed me as well just to make the whole picture complete.

What happened then was that Mary came and placed me between her and Dad as a human shield, third party. I was her witness to the scratch marks on her throat and neck. She continued to harass him and I distinctly remember thinking this to myself, "Woman this is not the time to nag and badger, won't you shut up before we all get killed!" Dad eventually left that same night and soon afterwards the cops came and took their report and off they went. That was the end of the marriage between Dad and Mary.

My brothers came back home and we lived with Dad on the farm without Mary and I had a season of peace, but not for long. This time my own brothers set forth terms for me in which I had no choice, but to abide under or else face the music of their anger. By now we were all older and we had a reputation as being referred to as the "three little pigs". I can tell you the biggest "oinks" were them and not me! I became their "test pilot" for any and all projects they invented to test as to whether or not it was workable, I hated every minute of it. For several years we did things on the farm in total freedom of parental supervision to speak of. Dad was either working or spending his "off time" in the local tavern. Then Dad did the worse thing to us kids we could think of, he remarried but that is not all, the woman he married had five kids and all of a sudden our world came to a sudden halt.

We were tossed into a ring with this new situation and once again my "pit" got deeper and wider. It was while in this new environment that I started getting into trouble with the law and spent many weeks in a juvenile detention center. School grades went to straight "F's" and held steady. If I ever got a "D minus" I figured I was improving. One by one my brothers left home for good, once again divorce set in and this woman, along with her children, returned back to where she had come from and now it was just me and Dad on the farm.

I was so glad to have my brothers out of my life and it

was during this time I lived free of all the fear of what my brothers had been doing to me, for they had governed with a strong hand. I had to learn how to lie and lie well in order not to get into trouble. If Dad ever caught my brothers doing something wrong and their trouble occurred due to my failure to properly cover for them then that meant beatings. If I was ever caught in a lie by Dad then that too meant beatings from Dad. So I was in a "no win situation." If I ever told on my brothers, (which I never did), then I knew that too would mean payback. So it was a welcomed time to finally see my brothers leave and I could now be free.

This freedom soon generated another type of fear that I had not known before. What followed next was more than I could stomach. As far as the farm went, it was now run down and broken; we had no animals or gardens, all of that had long since died out. The farm was just a place to sleep, eat and get up the next day and go to school.

Dad continued his life as before, it was work and tavern for him. He would call from work and check in with me to make sure I was ok. I think it was his way to relieve his conscience for leaving me alone on the farm. Whenever he called, it was to make sure I was home from school and right before I went to bed. Each time I told him the same things, "Yes I have done my homework, yes dinner dishes are done, and yes, I will lock the house when leaving tomorrow". I was not ok, not at all, but yet I dared not really confess to him my true thoughts for Dad, (in my opinion), would not be able to cope with it because that would mean his conscience would be pricked and, in his guilt, I would be laughed at as being weak. I learned to live within a masked shell, never telling the truth but only giving Dad the answers he expected from me.

In those days, time dragged on like a slow consuming monster, I had no chance of getting free of its fangs; it just kept chiselling away at me, piece by piece, moment by

moment. Many nights I sat in the front room in the dark
scared to go to bed. I would let the dogs in the house and sit
on the couch looking down the hallway making sure no one
came in the back door. Night after night I would sit there on
the couch holding on to the loaded gun that lay across my
lap, waiting for some one to leap out at me from behind a
door. In the darkness of those lousy nights my imagination
gave me no rest from fear. Eventually I would end up going
to bed and the next day the whole process began again. When
Dad would call in the morning before leaving for school, my
words to him were something to this effect, "Yes dad, I had
a good night, I will call you when I get home today, bye."

Looking back on those years I now wish I had done
things differently, but its water under the bridge now. I will
say this in passing, the best time of my life as a kid was on
the farm and the endless hours I spent roaming the woods
with our dogs and my hunting rifle. While exploring the forest I had no set borders, I went everywhere. Every deer trail,
meadow, water hole, tall tree, wild animal and beaver pond
I mapped out and claimed it as my property. While there I
was free from my brothers along with fighting between parents and all the madness that resulted from it. While there I
was able to contact information from life that no school
book or teacher could impart to me. It was there I could have
stayed forever, and never looked back, but that was not
meant to be. This seemed to be the completion of my "pit
digging," At the age of sixteen, all alone on the farm and cut
off from what was happening in the world, I decided I have
had enough. So I did the only thing that seemed to be my
best exit, I ran away from home.

Chapter Three

Miry Clay

At the age of sixteen I did what I had wanted to do for some time now, I ran away from home. For the entire summer I lived on the street and slept under bridges or wherever else I could find to bed down. This was quite a summer for me and even though I sometimes carried a fear of running into Dad, or getting "busted" by the cops, the freedom I felt in comparison to the farm was like heaven on earth. I had no-one to tell me when to go to bed or when to get up, all of that was over with. This freedom was like no other that I had experienced before and I enjoyed it very much. Of course, with a new situation there also came some unforeseen problems such as lack of clothing, laundry, etc. Even so I was able to adjust and learn how to live and later survive quite well.

Unknown to me at this time, I was on "miry clay" as far as thinking I was away from my problems. In reality, the very things I started to engage in were nothing more than being on the sides of a slippery slope. Drugs, for example, took me into places I had never been and I was very deceived by their use into thinking I was now finding happiness and well- being. Yet, I was only slipping and sliding into the deep abyss as fast as I could go. More and more there became an obvious emptiness inside me that would never go away, but kept coming back to haunt me at night when I was alone under the bridge. It was during those times I would lay there and think about my life and how things were for me. My biggest battle was throwing my outward conscious man against the inner voice in the hope of bringing to pass some kind of reasonable and acceptable living arrangement with both parties. However, since this was a "God thing" I could never get a handle on being successful.

During the day time I would awake and make my way downtown to "panhandle" for money and talk to other street kids. Hour after hour I would spend just hanging out and living free. As long as I had my freedom I was ok, but always at night I continued to be harassed by inner conscience that would not let me alone to enjoy my life. Sundays were rough, for not many kids would be hanging out on the streets until much later on in the afternoon. As a result I would just walk around and pass time by looking at the many display items in store fronts, waiting for things to happen.

I met girls who taught me things I had never known before and love was encountered for the first time that summer. Even this carried no real lasting bond and I wondered why it was so fun, yet so empty at the same time. I saw other kids who were taking drugs and using needles. I tried that too, and all the while I walked along that path God was keeping me safe from harm. However, not once did I consider Him in those days unless I needed Him for help or deliverance. I saw kids from rich homes that had no reason to be on the street, yet they too, were slipping on their own slopes. I saw young girls who hung out on the streets wanting to be part of this new movement, but at night they went back home as if it was no big deal. I saw death during that summer, it seemed to me that love and death were partners connected together in order to prevent me from having any joy.

The summer passed and when the nights started to get cold and the fall was chasing the warm days away I got "busted" for drugs and was sent to jail. For the next two years I was in juvenile reformatory, and when I turned eighteen I was placed on adult parole and released from jail. By this time, I had developed a track record of making a mess of things and it was only a few weeks or so later that I broke my parole. The minute I did so I knew I would be sent to Walla Walla State Prison when, or if, I was picked up by the cops.

For all of my life I had been told what I needed to do in order to be normal, yet a rebellion would rise up within me and would reject all such advice from those who attempted to "make me like them." My Dad, for example, at one time said to me, "Why don't you be like me?" I knew he meant well, but I could not tune into what he was saying for I only saw in him the life he lived and the failed marriages. I remember at that time thinking this to myself, yet I dared not tell him my thoughts. I wanted no part of following his life as a standard of operation in which to function. There was no question that I was lost. However, I knew Dad was also missing something too. My eldest brother also attempted to help me with his advice by trying to instil within me a family pride. Once, while sitting in juvenile jail, he came to visit me and he said, "You are from a family of good standing; you don't have to live like this." The first thought that came to me was, "yeah right!" As it turned out I was unable to live up to that advice either.

So on that day, while considering my circumstances with the parole violation, cops, prison, and my life with all of its twists and turns, I made a conscious decision to leave my town and find answers to life. I said to myself "if there is something out there I will find it, if there is meaning to life and some kind of sense as to what is going on I will either find it or whatever." With that I headed out of town hitch-hiking south in hope of a better tomorrow.

Chapter Four

Life on the Streets

"And you hath he quickened, who were dead in trespasses and sins; Wherein in time past ye walked according to the course of this world, according to the prince of the power of the air, the spirit that now worketh in the children of disobedience: Among whom also we all had our conversation in times past in the lusts of our flesh, fulfilling the desires of the flesh and of the mind; and were by nature the children of wrath, even as others." (Ephesians 2:1-3)

This next section of my life is like an insane dream. Had I known what things would have been like for me upon leaving my home town, I would have stayed at home. In less than two short years I had dug my personal "horrible pit" about as deep as it could go. By my own actions, I wiped out any and all hopes of living a productive, successful life, as normal people strive to do. Personally, I would rather not even write on this portion of my life for it is such a time of darkness and waste. However, I will quickly touch on a few areas and then move on to healthier situations.

While hitch-hiking from Washington to California I was given a ride by a fellow who was heading to a commune in Northern California. My first encounter with people was when I arrived there with him. This particular commune was everything and more for me to experience. There were all kinds of people and all kinds of things to do.

It seemed to me, that due to the age of some of the folk on this particular commune, many of them appeared to be some of the "fathers" of the establishment of the so called, "hippy movement." However, the ideas they embraced and promoted were nothing but high sounding nonsense. Peace and love were just illusions of dead-end fancy notions. These notions had no way of getting off the ground due to the sin-nature that continued to work in the back ground of human lust and selfishness. The obvious, (but not realized at that time), was the "upside down cross factor."

The famous peace sign that flapped in the winds of change over the heads of the youth culture was, in reality, a symbol of rebellion and wickedness, directly aimed at usurping God's authority within the lives of mankind. Once again the age-old deception was alive and well in the 50's and 60's. It is a common practice of Satan to usher in his programs by way of social acceptability and the "peace and love" slogan seemed to be innocent and worthwhile. Yet, it was a disguise for that which lay hidden right below the surface. Hitler's Germany also had its day in the sun when it flew the flag of Nazism over the world, but in true reality it was a war with spiritual implications.

Too often we give acceptance to programs or good sounding ideas based merely on outward appearances, yet never bother to dig deep into the unseen departments of deception and lies. As a result, therefore, many innocent people become victims of new agendas that later bring suffering and bondage after the nature of the beast is revealed. This style of "angel of light" still works today and we can see it woven throughout the world within all fabric of governments, special interest groups, political and social environments, human rights groups and individual people. To draw on a personal example of this thought, I am reminded of a situation that I encountered several years later concerning deception based on outward acceptance.

I had just got off work for the night and was downtown waiting for the bus ride home. I had some time to kill so I went into a place known as the "Plaza." While there, I saw a well dressed lady who looked quite professional. She was handing out pamphlets to whoever would take one. My style was to investigate what she was doing, so I began to ask her questions concerning her program. She was offering a self-help program to young drug users with the hope of offering them a better way to live. Now in itself that is all fine and dandy, yet as we talked I turned the conversation to Christ and the need to establish who He was. She insisted that Jesus was merely a "good man" who was a source of "light," but only one "light" of many "lights" to the "father." Well I had heard that before and I did not buy that as being truth. In my awkwardness I let her know that Jesus was the only Son of God and there was no other. I guess that must have hit home with her for instantly her temperament changed radically towards me. Her true character beneath her fancy clothes and polished face became apparent. All of a sudden she went into a crouching position, like a cat getting ready to jump on its victim. Her hands stretched out like claws and she circled me saying, "I know who you are." So there we were in the plaza late at night, going round and round in tiny circles, like a jungle war game. To make a long story short, she left after a few minutes and I got on the bus and that was that. The point here is to investigate the inner motives by introducing the gospel to the established outward agenda. If the foundation is sure then "light" will embrace "light," but if the hidden things are of darkness then the "light" will reveal bad connections.

While in this commune I saw first hand the forces of darkness working behind the scenes, bringing to pass demon activity and possession. Mind altering drugs were the tools that opened inquiring minds to the demons and occult world of that day. I stayed there for about two or three months. When I finally left I was not the same anymore. I drank from a cup of self-indulgence and as a result much personal damage occurred while taking the drugs that were so widely available at that time. I left the commune and entered into another world, within my world of nothingness. It was at this stage of my life that I began living on the streets. This included hitch-hiking over a wide area of the United States. I have been asked by close friends what my life was like during that time and how I survived in those days.

Street life boils down to a bare bottom line, one word describes it in a nutshell, "survival!" That is all there was left for me at that time. Each day the routine of food, sleep and lust was all that I had to maintain. As far as a future there was none to look forward to for my life revolved around my own world and nothing else mattered. I did not care for anything but what I could get out of each situation. I learned to manipulate, con, push and pull to get what I wanted. With that as my basis for survival I had to set aside conscience and sympathy along with compassion. To flourish on the streets I had to be callous regarding how and what I used as tactics to fulfil my daily routine and this was the pattern that I lived under. It consumed my whole life and reduced me to an animal mentality which offered no future or benefits, but meant constant effort to get by from day to day.

Chapter Five

The Cleansing Blood

"But God, who is rich in mercy, for his great love wherewith he loved us, Even when we were dead in sins, hath quickened us together with Christ, (by grace ye are saved;) And hath raised us up together, and made us sit together in heavenly places in Christ Jesus: That in the ages to come he might shew the exceeding riches of his grace in his kindness toward us through Christ Jesus. For by grace are ye saved through faith; and that not of yourselves: it is the gift of God: Not of works, lest any man should boast. For we are his workmanship, created in Christ Jesus unto good works, which God hath before ordained that we should walk in them. Wherefore remember, that ye being in time past Gentiles in the flesh, who are called Uncircumcision by that which is called the Circumcision in the flesh made by hands; That at that time ye were without Christ, being aliens from the commonwealth of Israel, and strangers from the covenants of promise, having no hope, and without God in the world: But now in Christ

Jesus ye who sometimes were far off are made nigh by the blood of Christ. For he is our peace, who hath made both one, and hath broken down the middle wall of partition between us; Having abolished in his flesh the enmity, even the law of commandments contained in ordinances; for to make in himself of twain one new man, so making peace; And that he might reconcile both unto God in one body by the cross, having slain the enmity thereby: And came and preached peace to you which were afar off, and to them that were nigh. For through him we both have access by one Spirit unto the Father." (Ephesians 2: 4-22)

B y this time I had exhausted what little chance I had to climb out of the "pit" I had dug in my personal life. My health was going out the door due to abuse and more abuse. My head was caving in and "voices" within were telling me things that left me almost powerless to resist. I guess the best way to sum it up is by saying that I was going insane. However, God was still there and I was under His watchful eye with each step that I took. The God I prayed to in times of trouble was the same God who walked with me during my times of neglect and rebellion. Throughout this time I wanted my way and I insisted on doing things that cemented my own selfish desires and whims. Little did I know that the God I had heard about and talked to, was soon going to reveal to me just who He really was.

I must now bring attention to this truth. It must be realized that a person's mental condition does not hinder God's Spirit from reaching him or her. Too often we might be thinking that unless someone is capable of understanding the gospel through human brain capabilities then they can be saved. If that is the case, then those who are dysfunctional through mental retardation have no hope of knowing Christ and entering into forgiveness of sin and newness of life. Nothing can be further from the truth in that regard. In my own case, I had worn my brain down to the point that I could not function properly as a human being. However, I was still under God's dealings and it made no difference to Him whether or not I was mentally "right" to be saved or not. We are not to judge or withhold the gospel due to who we consider to be reachable. God's Spirit is the one that reaches high and low within each person's life. He touches the heart and brings about change.

In October 1970 I found myself in Spokane, Washington. I had been hitch-hiking now for a long time and during this time I had returned back from time to time. On one occasion, upon entering town, I met a former high school kid who was by then a Christian. Upon meeting me, he instantly shared how he had come to Christ. I had heard testimonies from others before. However, this time his testimony had a different effect on me for I knew him as a former high school buddy. Due to this knowledge I was not able to dismiss his testimony as fake. God had His hand in this encounter and this man invited me to go with him to Seattle to a place called "Teen-Challenge." The strange thing was I agreed to do so. It was way out of character for me to commit to such a thing, so looking back, God had His hand in these events that were coming at me from out of nowhere.

We arrived in Seattle the next day and went straight to the Teen Center. I remember the trip there as one filled with regrets; I wished I had never agreed to go. I felt trapped while sitting in the back seat, staring out of the car window watching the boring landscape go swiftly past as we drove on and on. My former class mate along with another "Jesus man," talked about Jesus from the time we left Spokane to the time we got to Seattle. If that was not bad enough, every time I attempted to smoke a cigarette, they both suddenly stopped talking about Jesus and instead spoke on things that made my smoking very unpleasant.

Finally we arrived at our destination and I was taken to the front office. The staff introduced me to the program and also explained the rules and regulations under which I was expected to abide. This instantly presented a major problem for I was not prepared for this loss of freedom. In less than two hours I had broken two rules and was taken to the office for a final warning. This was more than I was able to endure and I walked out. That was the end of my long stay there and by now it was around five in the afternoon.

My freedom to move about and do whatever I wanted had been my "guiding star" for some time now and I was just not able to give this up immediately. I had learned to take advantage of situations by pretending I was serious. Yet, when it boiled down to making commitments or being confronted with deciding to live for Christ, that was another story all together. So when these people cornered me over giving my life to the Lord, I made my exit, which was my style.

Once again I was alone and had to scramble about to figure out how to survive through the night. It was getting late and I was walking towards the heart of Seattle's downtown district. Suddenly I had this overwhelming feeling of being lost and miserable. My life started flashing across my mind and it left me with a huge sense of emptiness and despair. I stopped walking and went into a phone booth that was nearby me at the time. It was there I tried desperately to find the phone number to the teen challenge office, but that was a waste of time. So while in the booth and under the heavy weight of sorrow and emptiness I said this prayer. "God, my life is going nowhere and I have heard about you from many people throughout the last year or so.

I am tired and worn out and I would rather die than live like I have been living. I don't care what happens to me from now on. If you are here and if you are leading me, then I ask that you control my feet and send my legs to where you want me to walk."

I left the booth and started walking without even caring where I went. It was now ten o'clock at night and I was downtown. Suddenly I heard singing coming from somewhere ahead of me and I was propelled forward as if drawn by a magnet. There were two ladies singing on a street corner about the love of God. I stopped and listened to their singing and the words and the music reached out like a blanket and surrounded me as never before.

The next thing I remember was that one of the ladies came over to me and started saying something about Jesus. I really did not hear what she was saying for it seemed that I was a million miles away. Right there and while many were walking by me on the street corner, I reached my hands toward the sky and said these words, "God if you are real, please tell me so!" This was the most important question that was on my heart. I needed to know if He was real or not. Reality for me was fleeing fast and everything seemed to be illusionary and blurry.

The very next event that took place changed my life completely. I suddenly felt a physical sensation of warmth moving over me from somewhere deep inside. This feeling grew bigger and bigger. Then it vanished leaving me with a sensation of "cleanness" as I had never felt before. If that was not enough, a peace unlike anything I had ever felt before came over me and my world took on a new direction from that day forward. Later, I came to realize I had been "Washed in the Blood" and made clean from within. I will never forget that day, it was October, 1970.

If I thought for a moment that my life would continue on as before I was in for a huge surprise. My story did not end there, but rather it was just the beginning of a ride that was soon going to take me to places and changes that can only be defined as a "God thing."

Chapter Six

New Wine Old Wineskins

"No man putteth a piece of new cloth unto an old garment, for that which is put in to fill it up taketh from the garment, and the rent is made worse. Neither do men put new wine into old bottles: else the bottles break, and the wine runneth out, and the bottles perish: but they put new wine into new bottles, and both are preserved." (Matthew 9:16-17)

T he Seattle incident did not end with me just being saved and then turned loose to stumble through the rest of my life. Instead, I now had become God's property and I can say that He took very seriously His ownership over me that had been purchased by the very life blood of His Son on my behalf. On that night new life had been conceived within me, however, the old wineskin was still very much in need of replacement and the process of renewal was exactly that, a process. I was not only in major need of healing, but also I had some habits and controlling patterns that needed to be dealt with. Life for me was not, "business as usual." I wish I could say I entered into my salvation in working order, but unfortunately I was disjointed and in need of major repairs. It is not surprising to me when Jesus referred to putting "new wine in new wineskins" that I may have been the example he was quoting.

The two ladies soon found out that I was homeless, but not for long. They took me to a place that same night and the following morning I attended my very first church service of the "real thing!" It was like no other church that I had been in before with singing and much excitement all over the place. In fact, the two ladies that led me to the Lord were also there and they were just as happy then as they were on the previous night. I sat on the front row and was as stiff as a board while the whole place was super-charged. It was hard to hide in the crowd when they were acting differently than me, but I tried my best to act like I was not a "dry twig" in the "raging forest fire." However, my attempt to do so was ineffective. At the close of the service the pastor gave an alter-call for anyone who wanted or needed prayer. I was not the only one in church that morning, yet he kept looking right at me when he asked for someone to come forward. Well, he saw I was not going to move so he then did the next best thing and asked everyone to come forward. I was part of "everyone" so I joined the stampede. I will leave you to draw your own conclusions as to whom this man prayed for that Sunday morning.

I stayed around there for about three days and then the old habit of rebellion came once again. The pastor offered me the chance to attend a five month long college apparently connected with that particular congregation. Well, as I made mention to earlier, my old wineskin was not ready for new wine and I responded to the offer with a reverberating "no thank you". I shall never forget the change in his facial expression. It went from nice to not-so-nice almost about as fast as the word "no" hit his ear drum. I got up from the chair and left his study. It was Wednesday morning and time for me to hit the road again!

I continued to hitch hike, but now I had Christ in me and the things I did prior to His arrival were no longer any fun. I had no idea what sin was until that time nor did I have any bible knowledge or previous spiritual training to speak of. I soon discovered that it was very hard to enjoy the cheap thrills of sin owing to such a strong consciousness of the company of God all around me. I had made a few attempts at living my life before the Seattle salvation incident as if nothing had happened. However, I quickly learned that things were not the way they used to be.

The new life I now had was not going to just disappear, but it stayed with me for the long haul. I guess I figured it would leave after awhile, for in times past I experienced a type of peace. However, it was drug induced and in the morning things were back to the same old ways like smoke fading in the air. Naturally I assumed that this "Jesus peace" would also be like that as well, but praise God, it never did. Instead this peace I now enjoyed was a steady, calm, and a keeping peace that remained like a gentle breeze giving my soul freedom from worry and fear. Later on I began to learn how to use this peace like a compass setting in my life which really came in handy during some important decisions I needed to make.

I left Seattle and headed south once more. Wherever I went I kept running into God's people, and they would give me a place to stay for the night, which was really nice. It did not take too long for me to hitch-hike from Seattle to Northern California, but when I got as far as Eureka, once again the Lord began to speak to me concerning some things that I needed. In the exact same way a huge emptiness overshadowed me like it did while I was in Seattle. This time however, my need was not focused on being lost and unsaved, but rather the need of my heart was for me to have a place to live. While standing there on the south end of town waiting for another ride I spoke to the Lord and to this day I can still remember what I said and the words that I used. "Lord something happened to me in Seattle, I have a peace and a sense of your presence, yet I don't have a clue as to what I am doing or where I am going. I do know though that I can't just keep wandering around and hitch hiking. Lord I need to get to a place where I can learn of this life that is now in my possession. Lord you know my background and my upbringing as a child. I need family Lord and I need a place to learn and time to understand without having to worry how to live from day to day. I need moms, dads, uncles, aunts, brothers and sisters. Lord I need what I never had as a child, so Lord I ask that from this moment on that you lead me to a place and provide what I have asked of you."

That prayer came from inside me and I learned something important and useful that day. The Lord first of all knows what we need long before we ask Him, even better than we know ourselves. We might think we know what we need, but in truth we do not really know. If what we think we need and what we really need are not in tune with God's program, then we are way off base in the so called "need department." In my case, my true need was placed upon my heart and it was from that place of identification that I verbalized my need before the Lord. When I apply prayer before the Lord it needs to come from the connection of what is on my heart, in order for that request to carry any kind of substance before the Lord. I can always tell when the prayer is heard by the peace that has been replaced after the burden is lifted.

Peace always gets overshadowed by intense burden. I know that the greater and more crushing the burden is upon us, is when we need to pray harder and with more intensity. Sometimes our prayers will be nothing more than a "deep groaning" from inside. However, all burdens will lift after prayers and if we can not lift the burden ourselves then we need to employ other members of the body of Christ to enter the work place and help us in praying until the job is completed. Once the weight lifts then sweet peace once again embraces our spirit and we are free to go, trusting the Lord and enjoying His closeness. This is good teaching and can be applied in all areas of our Christian prayer life. So I said those things to the Lord on that morning and on that very same day at seven that evening my prayer was answered.

My old wineskin was beginning to undergo change. The process was one of the hardest times of my life. It truly is a fearful thing to fall into the hands of a living God. My life was no longer my own, yet I tried to take it back time after time.

Chapter Seven

A New Home

"Unto thee, O Lord, do I lift up my soul. O my God, I trust in thee: let me not be ashamed, let not mine enemies triumph over me. Yea, let none that wait on thee be ashamed: let them be ashamed which transgress without cause. Shew me thy ways, O Lord; teach me thy paths. Lead me in thy truth, and teach me: for thou art the God of my salvation; on thee do I wait all the day. Remember, O Lord, thy tender mercies and thy loving kindnesses; for they have been ever of old. Remember not the sins of my youth, nor my transgressions: according to thy mercy remember thou me for thy goodness' sake, O Lord. Good and upright is the Lord: therefore will he teach sinners in the way. The meek will he guide in judgment: and the meek will he teach his way. All the paths of the Lord are mercy and truth unto such as keep his covenant and his testimonies. For thy name's sake, O Lord, pardon mine iniquity; for it is great. What man is he that feareth the Lord? Him shall he teach in the way that he shall choose. His soul shall dwell at ease; and his seed shall inherit the earth. The secret of the Lord is with them that fear him; and he will shew them his covenant. Mine eyes are ever toward the Lord; for he shall pluck my feet out of the net. Turn thee unto me, and have mercy upon me; for I am desolate and afflicted. The troubles of my heart are enlarged: O bring thou me out of my distresses. Look upon mine affliction and my pain; and forgive all my sins. Consider mine enemies; for they are many; and they hate me with cruel hatred. O keep my soul, and deliver me: let me not be ashamed; for I put my trust in thee. Let integrity and uprightness preserve me; for I wait on thee. Redeem Israel, O God, out of all his troubles." (Psalms 25:1-22)

Not long afterwards I received another ride and I headed south again. This particular ride took me to Berkeley, California. I was familiar with Berkeley since I had previously spent much of my street life hanging around the university. I just had an inner knowing that God was with me and that somehow or somewhere my prayer from that morning was going to be answered. As soon I arrived in Berkeley I headed towards campus and while there I stood around the university plaza waiting and wondering when the Lord was going to show me His will. As usual there was a lot to do. I waited and waited, but nothing seemed to be happening. I started getting serious doubts as to whether or not I was at the right place for God to come through on my behalf. One thing I had already determined and that was that no way was I going to ask anything from anyone. I was not going to be of any assistance in helping

God out either. I had come to a place where I did not want to feel that I had used my own will to make this God thing come to pass.

I waited and waited until two complete strangers walked up to me and invited me to a campus drug party. This was not uncommon, but for me the timing was bad. Usually I would not have given such invitations any hesitation, but this time I discarded both offers and continued to give God some time to work. After both of these encounters I started to have doubts as to what I was doing. I even began to consider forgetting God completely and living a life of sin and forgetting everything. I then said a silent prayer while standing on a brick wall overlooking the campus activities. "Lord, I came down here from up North and I am looking for the prayers to be answered. Yet, so far nothing has happened; in fact since I have been here all I am getting is offers to take drugs. I have rejected both of these and still nothing is happening. I don't understand it and it is getting late, so Lord I must be in the wrong place. I will now leave and hitch-hike into San Francisco, maybe while there you can show me what I need."

After this short prayer I got down from the wall and started to leave for good. Once again the sound of singing stopped me dead in my tracks. I heard what sounded like angels singing. This was just like another replay of the Seattle experience all over again. The Lord was using music to get my attention and make me change direction. I once again moved towards the sound of music and soon I was standing in front of a group of ladies. I stood off, watched and listened. I remember thinking how happy they were, but I was not going to ask them for help or tell them anything of my situation. After a few minutes I decided that nothing was going to happen so I turned to leave. I was leaving alright, and it may have been the last time for me to consider God ever again. I was almost out of the immediate area when I felt a light, but firm tapping of someone's finger on my right shoulder. God's timing on my behalf was just when I needed Him and not a minute too soon. I slowly turned around and looked into the face of a young girl who I did not recognize, but she knew me. Upon telling me who she was my memory of her returned again. She had come to Berkeley as a runaway some time ago and we had met on the avenue. She was not only running away from home, but also running from the Lord as well. So there we stood while she gave me a complete update on her happiness. She then told me that she was no longer a runaway nor was she away from the Lord either. She took me by the arm to come with her to meet not only her mom, (gulp) but her other friends who, as it turned out, were the singing Christians.

While being individually introduced I shook the hand of one lady who definitely had a "mom" type personality. She was also Italian and I should have known right then that I was in for some changes. It turned out I was right for she was a most loving and kind lady. As I continued to communicate with these people, the "mom" type of woman drew back and stood in the background and her lips were moving as if talking to someone, yet I could see no-one by her. God had spoken to her right after we were introduced and told her that I was to go with her to her place. She was in the corner of the singing area telling the Lord that she did not want to do that. The two of them, were having a serious conversation and I was the topic. She told me later, after I got to know her, that on that day she was trying to talk the Lord out of what He told her concerning me.

Once again events were happening like lightening. When I arrived at her house I was given basic introductions and a quick history of this home and what it stood for. It was called the "Fish House" which was a New Testament term with the reference being on Jesus feeding the multitudes with loaves and fish. The house was not only a private home, complete with mother, daughters, and a son, but also it was a home for those who the Lord sent for spiritual purposes. I was one of a long line of chosen vessels who abided under this home's ministry and received from God, the "Bread of Life." Not only did I get placed in a private home, but I was right in the middle of a church life with many active brothers who were keen on supporting this ministry. They took an active responsibility in discipleship by just being themselves.

In retrospect, these events and when I left Seattle under what appeared to be a rejection of God in my situation; I cannot say for sure if what I did up there was not part of the overall plan of God. Yes, we can hinder God's work by refusing to submit and being obstinate and pig-headed. However, it does not matter what we do, for God will get across His program and since He is God then He is in control of all wisdom and knowledge. Since He has made us and fashioned us out of nothing, but clay, then surely He can use any and all means to work in us things that shape and twist us into whatever He desires. As long as we have a heart for God and down deep in our Spirit we love the Lord and remain loyal and true, then with that material God can work out the details.

Chapter Eight

A New Foundation

"Being confident of this very thing, that he which hath begun a good work in you will perform it until the day of Jesus Christ." (Philippians 1:6)

I soon realized that I was in a new world right away and that God had brought me to this home and had placed me right in the middle of the very thing I had asked Him for. That in itself was so amazing to me and to consider it was so overwhelming that at times I just could not take it in.

After the first connection was established within my heart and life, then from that position the Lord began making other links which as a result ushered in growth. From that I slowly began to move off my salvation platform to other levels of growth, but the process was filled with a lot of downtime and fleshly blunders which made the job look hopeless at times.

One particular day when I was walking on the beach and enjoying the nearness of the Lord, I asked Him this question.

"You gave me lots of family yet I did not get a dad type of person and I don't know why not!" I have to admit that this bothered me enough to finally ask the Lord about this so that I could have some peace in place of misunderstanding. This is how it was in those days between the Lord and I, exchanges were made back and forth as to who I was and what His purpose was in my life.

It is better when in doubt over anything that we clear it up as soon as possible so we can then maintain completely open networks of communications between our God and us. If we instead dismiss such questions as not important then we miss out on hearing from the Lord regarding those things of which we have need. His reply back to me was as follows, "I gave you all that you asked for, however I did not give you a father figure, instead I will be your father and be to you that which in the past you did not have, you are my child and I am your Father."

Upon receiving that word from the Lord we entered into a father/ son bond that began to take shape and grow as we conversed together. Through this type of involvement the end result was a foundation in which to walk upon. However, the construction of this foundation was laid hard upon me.

Chapter Nine

Who Is In My Head

The Spirit itself beareth witness with our spirit,
that we are the children of God:" (Romans 8:16)

Upon arriving at this new home, it was there that
the abuse of my former life hit me pretty hard in
the area of my mental functions. My time was
spent just sitting in an orange recliner and not speaking very
much. About the only thing I could acknowledge other than
my name and age was that I was "saved." This fact was not
based on what I claimed, but rather it was confirmed by the
Spirit bearing witness to me that I was indeed a child of
God. God had His hand upon me even though I appeared to
be "out of it." Yet His healing abilities were not powerless at
restoring that which I had suffered by abusive "sowing and
reaping" projects that I had insanely partaken in. I do not
recall the days or weeks that I remained in this kind of condition, but I do remember that the woman in whose home I
lived talked with the Lord about me all the time. In her concern for me as a child of God she prayed and she offered me

love and faith which was in short supply on my own personal grounds.

This woman became known to me as "mom" and she told me that one day the Lord had spoken these words to her. "I will heal him, watch and see my work done before your very eyes." I had no idea for sure what that meant for I had never been healed of anything and in reality I did not even know what she was talking about. Sometime after she told me this, I was alone in the house still sitting in that same old chair. It began as a normal day for me. I would get up in the mornings and after daily chores I sat down and stayed there until dinner time. I suddenly became consciously aware of some kind of movement inside my skull. I can only describe it as a "little man" walking around in my head pulling things down and putting up new building materials. The sensations that moved around within my head were awesome to behold. My whole day seemed to be a day of mental construction and repairing.

I must point out that my head, will and emotions were separate points of future healings. The Lord covered all three, one by one over the next year or so. When the Lord heals He does not leave any stone unturned, but He does a thorough and complete job. I will share how the Lord worked each system out within my framework and how he was very patient with me, long after the patience of God's people hit bottom. Yet, He continued to hang in there and do what needed to be done.

That same day, mom came home from her place of work. When I had a chance to talk to her the first words were a testimony of what had happened to me. My exact words to her were, "There is a man inside my head hammering and tearing things down." Upon hearing me say this mom became very emotional and began praising more and more. This was the beginning of my healing and slowly over the next several months I was able to articulate once more and make intelligent sentences, instead of fragmented statements and broken thoughts.

I do not know how God did what He did, but I firmly believe that He removed the old junk out of my head and He "rewired" the circuits with a Spiritual understanding and insights that appeared as I began to read His word and absorb the Old and New Testaments. Day in and day out I spent hours sitting and reading, sometimes not even knowing what I was reading, yet it was shooting into the brain and from there it went into all compartments.

Chapter Ten

A Spinning Rat's Merry Go Round

"As a dog returneth to his vomit, so a fool returneth to his folly." (Proverbs 26:11) "But it is happened unto them according to the true proverb, the dog is turned to his own vomit again; and the sow that was washed to her wallowing in the mire." (2 Peter 2:22)

While at the house another event began to take place. I ran into a previous girl friend with whom I had been greatly involved and to my surprise she too was now a Christian. I introduced her to the house members and everything seemed to be going well for a season. However, it became quite apparent that I had made a good thing go bad by making this girl pregnant and in doing so the Lord stepped in and stopped the future plans we were making. The war between God and I began to escalate greatly. I fought hard on the battlefield, wanting my own way and as a result I came to meet a stiff opposition from the Lord as He began to deal with me with a strong hand. Has anyone ever been in that situation before?

One day while sitting on the front steps of my girlfriend's home I was mentally reviewing a plan of backsliding in which I would face the least amount of heart-ache and stress. While considering this project my girl came outside and together we sat and talked. What happened next was just one more example of the Lord putting His views on the subject at our feet.

There came a silly looking dog walking down the road in front of her house. We both had our eyes on him as he started to walk by the driveway, he then stopped, did a complete turn around and headed straight for me. Upon arriving at my feet it was there he presented me with vomit. From that loud, but understandable word from the Lord, His thoughts on my so called dazzling plans became apparent. My girl friend did not think much of them either. She got up from the porch, quoted a bible verse and went back into the house.

I wish I could say that the reality of the living Word presented to me was enough to change my direction. However, I was headstrong and I went head first into backslide, and left California heading back to my home town. While there I made so many errors and such a mess of things; even though God was speaking to me, I would not listen. The Lord had His hand on me, but like a rebellious child I ignored what He was saying.

"Whither shall I go from thy Spirit? or whither shall I flee from thy presence?" Psalms 139:7

I ran to get away from the inner sorrow that held me in its vice-like grip. During this time I went further and further into trying to bury that "still small voice within." This was God letting me know that He was still with me. On one particular morning I asked the Lord out of desperation concerning the circumstances surrounding me at that time, to show me His way. As usual His response was swift and to the point, "Go back to the house."

I knew exactly what that meant and once again a flood of guilt and condemnation poured into my soul. Part of my seeking to run from the Lord was based on the belief that these people would not allow me or want me back in the program. I just could not bring my weary failures back to face the fear of rejection. However, I did acknowledge the commandment that day and slowly turned around and hitch-hiked south. At that time I was about as far as I could go in the Northeast section of Washington State and Canada was only a few miles away.

What should have only taken a week of travel time turned out instead to take three months of hitch-hiking. Each day I traveled took up three days of downtime. I kept running into opportunities to partake of the things of the world and in my backslidden state I offered no resistance to such shallow pleasures. Yet, even in this time of spiritual darkness, God was with me waiting silently in the background. His Spirit was there every morning when I awoke, reminding me of my decision to head home. I continued moving south and finally I arrived within a few hours of my spiritual destination. I deliberately stopped for the remainder of the day in Mill Valley, California.

What happened next was nothing short of God, as well as the Devil, making clear to me the realities before me. I shall never forget the way it happened.

Chapter Eleven

It's Your Call

When I headed south from Mill Valley towards Pacifica, I had no plans on going further than the place where the Lord had long since instructed me to return. As I climbed out of my dirty sleeping bag I simply walked away from it, leaving it lying there along with the few clothes I had.

The very first ride I hitch-hiked was with a hippy fellow heading south. As it turned out he was heading all the way down the coast to Los Angeles. On the floor board of his car was a case of my favorite brand of beer and not only that this man was more than willing to share what drugs he was carrying. I knew as soon as I jumped in the car that once again I was in a position of another "party opportunity."

We drove across the Golden Gate Bridge and headed south towards Los Angeles. However, the town I was going to was only south of San Francisco. With the radio playing hard rock, I sat there in silence, staring out of the window thinking hard about what was going on. I had the strangest feeling that this ride was a "God thing" once again and I needed to figure out what He was doing. What lay before me were the same opportunities I had been encountering day after day upon my instruction from the Lord to return back home.

It was during my thinking that I heard these words in my ears. "You did not tell God when you would go home; neither did He tell you when you needed to be there. You have been gone this long, one more day will not matter one way or the other. Go ahead and put off the house appointment until tomorrow. Look at the fun you can have today and the nice sunny day ahead of you. Los Angeles is less than a day's hitch-hike from here; one more day surely will not change anything."

This argument had its good points and sounded reasonable to a degree. The wheels in my head began to rotate and churn over the thought process just handed to me. Once again there was more silence, and then another wave of words came to me yet from a different direction. These words were as follows, "I have been with you all the way since I first told you to go back home. You have taken several months, yet I was with you all the while. Now you are getting close to where you need to be. Yes, you can go ahead and put off your decision for yet another day. Yes, there is tomorrow as well, I have drawn you to this day and now you must decide what you want to do. So go ahead and have another day as you have been doing. I must say that I will be here as usual, but now you must realize that this day is not a sure thing for you. I will not guarantee your tomorrows, so go ahead if you want to, but do so at your own risk."

I had two opposite views to hash over and make a decision upon. My head was sending messages of interpretation to my will as to the logic and meaning of what both views meant. It was very clear as to where I stood and what choices and consequences might result from my decision. I had heard from both parties as to what was before me in terms of choices and now I was left alone to make my decision. It was my "call" and no-one could make it for me. I was under pressure, yet I remained silent as we went down the road getting closer and closer to the town where I needed to go.

There comes a time in ones life when we come to what I call, "a crossroad decision." I was now at that place. Both realities had made their case before me and I was free to choose which one to follow. I was actually resting between two worlds and my life hung in the balance. I could no longer tip the scales for I had used up all the weights I had been carrying for so long.

Chapter Twelve

Now You Have
Done It

Just ahead was the exit where I needed to be let off. I pointed this out to the driver and he pulled over and I got out. I remember the look on his face when I informed him to let me out. He looked disappointed as though he had been emotionally let down. He drove away going to whatever lay ahead and I stood there watching the car disappear out of sight.

Instantly I came under a verbal bombardment of the most negative thoughts I could experience. "You fool!" screamed the voice in my ear, "These people don't want you back, why do you waste their time? They don't want you there at the house, why don't you just realize that and leave them alone? The only reason they let you stay there is because they don't know how to tell you to leave!" On and on came the accusations and the ridicule. It had such a strong force upon me that even though the house was only a few city blocks away, each step that I took seemed like it would never end. In my heart I really knew I had done the right thing, but I have to admit I wondered if these people would actually receive me back or not. The voice of torment seemed true enough in what it was telling me and I marched forward with fear building over the thought of rejection.

Finally the moment of truth had arrived and I walked up the sidewalk that took me to the front door and knocked upon the door of the "Fish House." The door opened and it was David (mom's son) standing there. Without the slightest look of hesitation he invited me in as if it was only yesterday since I had been there. The screaming words in my ear stopped for the moment as I came in the house and sat down in my final resting place, the orange recliner. As I sat there in the living room David was in the kitchen cooking breakfast, no-one else was home at the time. Mom was working and the youngest daughter was gone too.

As I sat there I could hear David talking in the kitchen. He was carrying on about how good the Lord had been to him, yet his words seemed way off in the distance somewhere. I was reliving the events of the past several months and all the junk of the garbage I had collected was stinking up my insides. It began to fester and build more and more when something like a huge vacuum cleaner turned on within my heart. It all instantly disappeared and once again I felt a cleansing release and a freedom of soul.

The burden I had carried for so long was now history as the Lord in his loving mercy took the weight of my sin and sorrow once again and I had such wonderful peace. My world now had sunshine and blue sky.

Had these people told me to leave their doorstep and never bother them again, then I do not know where I would be today. Praise God, for instead, they reached out and showed me the love of Jesus once more. The weight of my sin and the guilt I carried over my lousy actions could have been enough justification for them to send me away. Yet, they did what the world does not do; they showed me instead, mercy and acceptance. It was wonderful to say the least.

The price I paid for my wayward ways had put me in debt and when it came to pay-day I could not afford the price for the damages which had occurred, but once more I was brought to understand that Jesus in His mercy had already paid for all I had done. Even so I had consequences of all I had been engaged in. From that day forward a dark chapter in my life had come to a close. However, my story does not end there, but instead it began. The only thing that came to a close was my careless and flippant attitude towards the Lord and His people. I was given just enough rope to hang myself with and now I was exhausted and repentant of my backsliding and rebellion.

I shall never forget what a brother told me later on after being back home for a while. He said, "If you commit your life to Jesus you won't have the kind of troubles you have now." A year before I would not have understood what his words meant, but on that day I knew the wisdom of such a statement. On that day I made my commitment to Jesus and upon doing so I sealed my life and I placed within His hands my future. Much can be said concerning commitment. I have learned the hard way just how important commitment is in following Jesus. It is one thing to be saved and on our way to Heaven, but without commitment, service to Jesus is like driving a car with two flat tires.

Our level of commitment or how much we profess to love the Lord will be tested in order to see if we are truly what we say we are. Such was the case with me too. I had just returned back to the house and I had made my much needed decision to walk away from the loose living I had been engaged in. I was enjoying the presence of the Lord once more. In my heart I knew this time things were different for me. I had made my decision and there was no more turning back.

The Lord had one more test for me to go through before the work of His foundation under me could get started. Little did I know how important this test was going to be, yet it proved worthwhile to the Lord and without it the events that followed would have not taken place.

Chapter Thirteen

Testings To Blessings

"Being confident of this very thing, that he which hath begun a good work in you will perform it until the day of Jesus Christ." (Philippians 1:16)

Now that I had finally made a commitment to service for the Lord things were much different. This commitment was more than just "lip service." In order for it to be sealed as genuine, God placed me in a situation where my heart was tried to see just how real I was going to be. In times past I failed the most elementary tests due to a lack of commitment. My dedication in those days always came up short at my end of the bargaining table.

Here is something we need to get a solid grip on if we are ever going to make spiritual progress in our walk with the Lord. Our statements about how dedicated we are are great and should be encouraged at every turn. However, God is not fooled by great or lengthy speeches. He knows the heart and it is there that He directs His attention. Before blessings can arrive in our life, the Lord, as the Master Builder, will spend time in preparing the foundation code. The testing at that stage is merely to ensure that the blessing of building substance can stand without falling.

God had begun a good work in me, but the complete building process of that work was tested and delayed at times over the issue of foundations. Without a solid rock foundation under our feet the whole structure of the house is faulty and weak. When testing comes to check the foundation, if there are any weak spots or cracks, then the Lord will surely know soon enough and such was the case with me.

God knew my heart and even though I outwardly pledged my life to Him, yet at that time that pledge was not confirmed by a test. The test was necessary in order for the blessing to arrive. The Lord desires to bless his children with a firm and strong house of character and strength, yet without first proving the underlying foundation the blessing will be put on hold.

Maybe it appears that I am repeating this thought over and over again. Well good, for I cannot say enough of just how important this truth is and how our whole Christian life swings on this principle. One reason I can talk of commitment with such authority and confidence is because I, myself, lived a life without it, both in the world and unfortunately also into my Christian life. A lack of commitment and dedication untested and unproven makes for a shallow relationship and surface showmanship. So with that said let me now share how one day shortly after my return to the house and my re-establishment to God's grace I encountered a test.

I was hitch-hiking home from Redwood City, California. I knew that the person who stopped to give me a ride was someone I never wanted to see again. I knew this fellow

was into drugs and I think he was also a dealer. Be that as
it may, the ride presented to me was another "God thing."
Instantly, upon getting into the car, I realized that once
again I was confronted with what I had already forsaken
and rejected a while back. I remembered praying to the
Lord as we drove towards the coast highway. I sat silent, but
the words I said were straight towards Heaven. "Lord why
are you doing this to me? I am not interested in living in the
world any more, why of all the people in this whole populated city did I have to meet this fellow?" On and on I
protested and wanted to know what the deal was before the
Lord. I could have been talking into thin air for all the good
it did as not once did I get any return words from the Lord.
Finally we got to the junction of the coast highway. He was
going south and I needed to head north. Another "crossroad
thing" and without once looking back and considering
whether or not which way to go, I got out of his car and
thanked Him for the ride. I rejected what He stood for and
walked away.

"I, the Lord, search the heart, I try the reins, even to give
every man according to his ways, and according to the fruit
of his doings. "(Jeremiah 17:10)

When I got out of that car and stood there I heard the
devil shout his mindless allegations, yet I was so above that
in my spirit. On that day and at that hour the foundation had
been tested from one end to the other and no cracks, blem-
ishes or rot was found to exist. My feet were upon a rock and
from that day forward, never again did I have to go through
a test to see if I was who I said I was.

A final chapter in my life ended yet another new chapter
was now being written. The stages of my life were exactly
that, stages and what was now to come was brought to me in
ways beyond my wildest dreams.

I made a pact with the Lord on that day, one of praise and
stronger dedication to His work in my life. I loved the Lord

and even though I was small in knowledge, yet I was large in purpose. I was set free on that day from a cycle of spinning round and round.

Chapter Fourteen

Established
My Goings

"But the God of all grace, who hath called us
unto his eternal glory by Christ Jesus, after that
ye have suffered a while, make you perfect, sta-
blish, strengthen, settle you. To Him be glory and
dominion for ever and ever. Amen." (1 peter
5:10-11)

There came a time on that particular day when I no
longer cared if my decision to refuse this world's
goods caused offence within the mind or heart of
he who was making the offer. I did not have any of the guilt
that I had in times past. I knew I was finally free to refuse that
which was not good because I had something much better
now. There was no way I was going to be pulled back into the
darkness of the world's holding tank of sin and sorrows.

I was not given the pleasure of spending endless hours
sitting around at the house as I had done in the past. My

mental state had been healed sufficiently enough that I no longer required isolation and shelter. I began to move about the area locally and at that time I shared Christ with the local teenage girls that were ever present. As a result of this, one by one, most of these girls came to the Lord and to this day are in service to Him. God was honoring His word as I seized the opportunity to testify to what He had begun to do within me.

Street witnessing was my favorite thing to do. It was as natural to me as breathing and I enjoyed it very much. So much, in fact, that whenever I had the chance I headed to downtown San Francisco and shared the Lord with the many people who were there. The Lord used me in spite of my imperfection and lack of tact. I would stand on street corners in the busiest sections of the city holding my bible. I noticed that the Bible in sight of the market place of human activity, with all of the spiritual forces of darkness within the meeting places of the city, would be the only tool I needed to engage someone in a conversation. I never knew from one day to the next what to expect. There were so many people and within the masses there were groups, as well as individuals, who were attempting to proclaim other messages rather than the truth found in Christ. On one such occasion I encountered a man who illustrates my point in this comment.

I had arrived at downtown San Francisco around midday and there were the usual tourist summer activities around the intersection of Market Street down by the Union Square. Within this scenario stood a man who was repeating bible verses from the Sermon on the Mount, found in the gospel of Matthew. Upon seeing this situation, my first thought was that this was great, a brother; I would stand nearby and pray for him as he preached. It did not take long before I got a definite sense that something was not right with this fellow. I then stopped praying and asked the Lord to show me the truth over what was going on. Discernment came immediately and from that vantage point I stood there and watched the drama unfold before me.

The fellow was quoting from the Sermon on the Mount, but the problem was that he was not quoting it in the manner of a Preacher. He was saying the words as if he was the creator of them. He paced back and forth and occasionally would look my way and see my bible in my hand, but continued speaking for some time. In the meantime I began searching the scriptures for confirmation of that which I had discerned just for a back up weapon. My first verse in light of revelation was very fitting and left me in no doubt that what I had felt in my spirit was Truth and Light.

"And Jesus answered and said unto them, Take heed that no man deceive you. For many shall come in my name, saying, I am Christ; and shall deceive many." (Matthew 24: 4-5)

Here was the truth as it stood on that day. Soon this man walked up to me and got right down to the purpose of his visit. He wanted to know why I had a bible and what I was reading. This was not an easy thing for me to do since I had no idea what kind of reaction would generate from my return comment.

However, there was no way I was going to just disappear and pretend everything was ok. I said to him, "Please read this verse that is in Matthew," I handed him the Bible and pointed out the verse where Jesus talked of many proclaiming to be Christ. After he had read this portion he handed me back the Bible and asked me why I had asked him to read that verse. I wish he had not asked me that. It would have been better had we started talking about the weather or shared fishing stories, but not so this time.

The ball was now in my court and he stood there with all his attention upon me waiting for my answer. I was new at this type of one-to-one conversation, not to mention that I was a little on the scared side. I looked at him and said, "I was watching you for awhile and I was going to pray as you preached. Not long afterwards I saw that you were not right and I turned to the Lord for some answers and this is what He showed me in His Word here. I see this verse is talking about you sir!" "Are you saying I am a false Christ?" he shot back! "Yes," I said.

At that point we stopped talking and he proceeded to make others, who were standing by, aware of my judgment and my sinful condemnation of him. He informed me that I had sinned against the Holy Spirit by not recognizing him as the "Christ." It became apparent that it was now time for me to leave.

Every situation and every encounter in our Christian life can give us insight into lessons learned that can come to us by such encounters. In this situation I once again took on the knowledge of truth. When we are given a revelation of reality from the Lord's position then that enlightenment ushers us into areas of action and responsibility. We act on what we are made aware of and our actions from then on will determine our faithfulness to service and accountability also. God does not hold us so much at fault with regard to how we respond to what we are made aware, in reference to how we go about bringing testimony to "light revealed". Yet, He does expect our actions to rise to the occasion once we are given insight into His word from that moment on.

Once we are made aware of truth then we are to witness that truth by living in the Light revealed from then on. Walking in the Spirit is best broken down in simple terms as meaning that we walk in the Spirit by walking in what we know. I now knew that once I saw the truth concerning this man on that day that I then proceeded on course from a new way of business. Furthermore, when I acted upon what I then knew it brought anger towards me over what I said. However, I was vindicated by the Lord, therefore, I was ok.

I continued to grow and learn while at the house, but things were changing in my personal life. How nice it would have been to remain free and easy going. However, the Lord once again began to work new things in respect of establishing my "goings" and enlarging under my footings a more secure foundation to stand on. How nice it would have been to live at the house under total freedom of movement and to witness on the streets without having a care in the world. Those days, however, were not meant to be for the Lord desired growth and maturity in which both were lacking at that time.

His hand was upon me and I was not going to be blessed by the Lord in a non-effort sort of way. It took effort on my part as I became obedient to those things He set before me to do. Things like getting up in the morning to attend a class to get my high school diploma or going to class every Saturday for a year to learn environmental landscaping skills and going to a doctor to get eye glasses.

These types of things may seem small and frivolous, however, to me; they were major happenings for healing came to me by action and that dreaded word, "responsibility." God was placing on my heart to begin to grow by way of jumping through "hoops." This goes back to what I made mention to earlier and that is that I could not stay in an easy going, "give-it-to-me" type of existence any longer.

I enjoyed the nearness of the Lord and the many times we walked together on the beach and talked. From there I received answers to my past, and the Lord was now bringing me to a place of changes by way of facing reality. In my dedication I openly accepted this new set of developments from the Lord. His will for me was what mattered most.

None of this was easy for I was on a collision course of two natures in one room. However, that was minor in comparison to having my world begin to shatter before my very eyes. The Lord was removing my comfort zones of security that I had become dependant upon during my stay at the house.

At the same time I was also learning other valuable lessons. I was able to associate my obedience to the impressions God was laying on my heart as the way to blessings. The Lord opened up doors and I was given opportunities to walk through them. In walking through these many doors and doing those things He had set before me I began to connect with strong cords of attachment with the Lord as a child in whom He could have confidence. This brought me much joy and all tasks seemed delightful instead of heavy and burdensome. It was my joy to do His will and to find His plan for my life. However, soon I was to face another situation which further escalated more changes and opportunities for deeper trust and reliance upon the Lord for direction.

Chapter Fifteen

The Closing
of the House

"Trust in the Lord with all thine heart; and lean
not unto thine own understanding. In all thy
ways acknowledge him, and he shall direct thy
paths. (Proverbs 3:5-6)

This verse soon became a living action in which to
apply to my life on a daily basis. Unless we come
to a place where the Word written becomes the
Word applied then what value is the Word to us? A mere
reading of the Bible without application of truth to daily life
brings no victory. In order for the Word to be proven we must
take the time to search out and see what the scripture means
and how we can best extract its total meaning and apply it in
order to grow from it properly, for example take this verse.

"Search the scriptures; for in them ye think ye have eternal life: and they are they which testify of me. And ye will
not come to me, that ye might have life." (John 5:39-40)

The key meaning to this statement by Jesus is as follows: We must come to Him in order to have life. Just reading the Bible without coming to Jesus is like trying to drive a car without a steering wheel. We take on a lot of head knowledge, yet no heart knowledge. The two need to operate together in order for the believer to be prosperous in the Word of God. Knowledge can either bring us closer to the Lord or it can drive us away. It all depends on how we approach knowledge and how we digest the information we glean from what we learn.

I have seen individuals with tremendous head knowledge when it comes to knowing the Bible and yet they have no idea of the most elementary teachings of Jesus when it comes to truth and relationship. Their knowledge is so elevated and puffed up that it collides with knowledge given by the Spirit and a person's walk with the Lord. In other words, these individuals are so filled with intelligence that when it comes to "truth" they cannot see beyond their educated knowledge therefore they resist truth and scoff at the gospel message as being foolishness. This type of knowledge is of little value, but knowledge that brings life and edification to another is learned by dealings from the Lord and from that position can then impart "life and Spirit" to those around us.

Such was also my case in application for one day Mom came into the living room after her morning prayers and announced that the Lord was closing down the ministry of the house and we, who lived there, had fifteen days to move out. At that time there were three of us living there.

Mom's announcement caused a certain stirring of thoughts as to what should we do now! Instead of getting all worked up over this news I recall at the time a supernatural sense of peace along with a feeling that this was the Lord's doing and everything would be okay. If anyone had a reason to panic I suppose I had the right to do so. The others who lived there had family close by so for them it was no big deal. In my case however, I had no-one to fall back on, neither turn to or call on. All the "props" under my feet were gone, so I did the only thing I could under the circumstances and turned to seeking the Lord for answers and direction. Like the common phrase I have heard quoted at times, "When all else fails, read the instructions." Seeking the Lord was the only solution to the events that demanded my attention in cases such as that which I was now facing.

Looking back on those kinds of problems I now see them as "blessings in disguise." As they appeared on the forefront of my life they drove me to seek God for direction which taught me many things in the process. During those times I connected with the Lord in ways that further strengthened my relationship which in turn caused me to have confidence in the face of future problems yet to arrive. The Lord sends things our way so we can learn to seek Him and secure a strong cord between Him and us. This is crucial for us as His children in these insecure times in which we find ourselves for He is the only anchor that holds.

While seeking the Lord I also continued to carry on my daily coming and going as the days passed. I continued to be free from worry even though the deadline grew nearer by the moment. David, (mom's son) was also taking it upon himself to get involved with the rest of us in this situation. He was under no obligation to move out since he was family, yet he too began making plans and at times took it upon himself to assume the leadership role in figuring things out and once again made a mess of things.

This type of planning by David presented a problem for me. At times I rebuked him for his lack of fully trusting in the Lord during those times. He was always presenting to us some new idea on where we all could live, but with each plan there was always came a flaw. In other words, an element of human reasoning to enter into the picture. I pointed this out to him as well as those around us which did not set well with him. However, it was necessary to establish the need to fully rely on the Lord and not upon our own merits. Being the kind of young man that David was, he did not receive this kind of rebuke well for it convicted him of his plans. The Lord used me at times to be a watchdog and sniff things out which of course had its own consequences. I can leave it up to the reader to decide how things went at times like that.

As often happens when one is convicted, frustration and anger over a rebuke is taken out on the one in front of them, namely me. However, that was ok for I was right in what I revealed over this kind of self-promoting which got in the way of doing the Lord's will. I held steady in what I knew was right even though I had no evidence to back up what I was insisting upon. In the end the Lord did come through and what He did for us all brought closure to the whole affair.

This is where the "tire meets the road" in the scriptural text of Proverbs 3:5. Too often we come against a change such as that which I was facing. We fall upon our own understanding on how to make things work and how to get around certain roadblocks by using less than honest means to acquire what we want. Then after the job is completed and our life is moving forward we then praise God for blessing us in such ways, yet during the process we ourselves did not once take the time to acknowledge the Lord in the paths taken to arrive.

In other ways we find ourselves in a situation that we do not like and attempt to deliver ourselves out from it by relying on our own understanding as the tool for such deliverance. We fail to realize that the Lord has us where we are in order for us to learn something, therefore we need to stay put until the lesson or lessons are learned and we grow.

I once had a boss who I did not like for valid reasons. Instead of remaining where I was and bringing the problem to the Lord, I requested to be transferred. I thought to myself, "Praise God I don't have to have this fellow as my authority any more." The following Monday upon arriving at work I ran into the boss from whom I had so skilfully fled. Unknown to me, he had also been transferred to the same location. In running ahead of the Lord I ran right into what I tried to avoid. So there I was, still under this man's authority and not liking it at all.

One day I headed to the Redwood City and the community college. While there I happened to be reading the notes and information on the bulletin board in the lobby. One particular note got my attention, even to the extent where I wrote the phone number down and actually called the place. The advertisement said they needed a "caregiver," of some kind. When I called I was given a time to come in for an interview. I had no idea then where this was going to lead, but the Lord knew. This was on Friday afternoon and the appointment was set for Monday morning. I had the entire weekend to prepare by having the Lord speak to me concerning whether or not this was His will and His leading. I told mom about it and she listened and got "that look" of happiness. I also went to church that Sunday and talked to the pastor's wife who also felt a sense of rightness over the matter. It was clear to me that the Lord was making a change and giving me an exit out of the house that I had come to enjoy. In some ways it was a sad event for it meant saying good-bye to the ones who gave so much of their time in helping me to adjust and overcome in so many areas of struggle and downtime.

Little did I know just how much the Lord had planned this change and how much my life was on the verge of a calling that meant sacrifices and healing from fear. My life up to this time was fairly easy and relaxed, but now that which lay ahead was soon to usher me into a new place where in order for me to survive I would require trust in the

Lord. With that at my side it was my time to say, "good-bye house, good-bye fellow brothers and sisters." Monday morning had finally arrived.

Chapter Sixteen

Breaking Free

"Be strong and of a good courage, fear not, nor
be afraid of them: for the Lord thy God, he it is
that doth go with thee; he will not fail thee, nor
forsake thee." (Deuteronomy 31:6)

I arrived at the house for my appointment which was
located in a quiet residential neighborhood and judging
by the appearance of the houses on the block this was a
well-to-do area. As I said earlier, I had no idea what kind of
work I was applying for. Maybe if I had known I would not
have applied, but there I was knocking on the door.

The door opened and there before me was a young man
in a wheel chair. My spirit froze within me and for a split
second I lost all my strength. This was not what I had figured on, but there he was and there I stood. We both made
eye contact and in that brief moment this fellow must have
read into my soul for I can only imagine the things He must
have seen in what my eyes revealed.

I had a definite problem with people who were deformed.
They scared me and I wanted nothing to do with them. It just

was not within me to get beyond the outward appearance of such people. It was easy to see that I did not have the kind of love mentioned in the Bible where it says, "There is no fear in love; but perfect love casteth out fear: because fear hath torment. He that feareth is not made perfect in love." (1 John 4:18) I was tormented by such appearances of this nature so naturally I fought against it by staying far away from people of such condition.

Just as fast as I froze up I instantly felt a surge of power from the Lord and in that power I received a dose of compassion which caused me to be able to reach out and shake his hand. He introduced himself as Laird and I told him my name. As we shook hands in greeting I felt a literal jolt of Spirit transmit from me to him like a current of electricity moving through power lines.

At that very moment the turmoil within me vanished and when I talked to him the words were not labored and strained, but rather genuine and real. This was great for I could now communicate without hiding my feelings. The connection I felt now was one of compassion instead of fear. It makes me wonder how often we talk from positions of fear towards those around us. Laird picked up on it too for I could see a look of surprise come over him as a result of it. We went on to finish the interview and by now I knew I was the man for the job. There was no doubt that the Lord was in it and in my mind there was no reason for further interviews. As was my style I told Laird that he may as well not have any more interviews since I was the one the Lord had sent to him for the job. I admonished him to be obedient and accept what was of God.

I had a way about me that at times might appear to others to be a little arrogant and conceited, yet in reality that is not it at all. Once I connect with the Lord's will concerning a matter, I then take on the role of making sure His will is established. As I said much earlier in previous chapters that

His will was top priority. As far as I was concerned, if others did not see it that way then we had a problem and the problem was not with me, but rather in their department.

Sometime politics and policy can interfere and get in the way of the Lord's will being fulfilled. Yet, I press on in the face of such barriers to bring to pass those things that hinder and delay the will of the Lord from being done. I remind those who struggle and protest to get their act together and "get with the program." In other words and in a more street version of saying it, "wake up and smell the coffee."

This same politic and policy problem is also found in church circles. When it comes to the Lord's will over church policy and procedure it is plain to see who and what is in control. If the truth was made known, we give "lip service" only when we claim we want the Lord's will to be first and foremost, but in reality man's ego is much bigger than he or she realizes.

Many spiritual dead-end roads result in not knowing the Lord's will in matters. We need to realize that before we can promote the cause of Christ we must first of all know His will both within us as well as in our surroundings. Once His will is imparted to our spirit that in turn ushers in boldness; this gives us confidence because now we have a direction.

The biggest problem swings on the fact that we are not too keen on being obedient to what His will is for us. We do not want to walk in the direction He points out because it will mean sacrifices and death to self. We cannot bring death to self without first of all having the Lord speak to us personally. Without Him giving us instruction and direction we have no road to walk on, therefore we lack purpose and vision. There is no joy in our Christian walk if we lack direction and purpose.

I went on to work as a "care-giver" in this family, and my whole life changed once more. I have to admit that it was not easy for me to be there. My personal freedom seemed far away and I also struggled over the shock of no longer being in a spiritual environment. The cold reality of no longer being with the family of God hit me like ice water! It was a time of growing and maturing and my life now centered on Laird. Whatever his day was to be; if he had an appointment to be at, then it was my job to go with him. I learned to pray in ways never before learned, many times my prayers were, "I can't do this!" It did not seem to matter to the Lord how many times I expressed my displeasure over what was required of me and not once did He "bail me out." He held ground against me and I always repented of my selfishness and stepped down off the throne and gave way to what He asked. I learned that at times the Lord places us in situations which seem hard to handle, yet He gives us the grace to get through them.

Laird and I spent many hours talking and during those times I began to see Laird as a person instead of a "deformed object." This too, was a healing time for me and as I yielded, the Lord in return, set me free of the chains that had held me for so long. In His wisdom the Lord had ordained me to be there for a season and a time of teaching which was in my best interest. I marvel at the way the Lord works in us. He brings us to a place of healing by way of placing us in certain situations where we have to trust Him and grow. It is not easy, but in the end we come forth the better as a result.

Even though this family were well-to-do financially they still had problems. Their money could not rescue them from the things of this world. The lady of the house was divorced and she had a boy friend who was a real sleazy fellow in my opinion. The youngest boy was a teenager in search of a meaningful life while the oldest boy was addicted to drugs. The grandma was a devout church attendant. It was in this atmosphere that I was placed and I felt it was my duty to bring the Lord to these people. Looking back on it now I see some of my mistakes and even some humor as well.

I was living in this house on a full time basis having one day off a week which was Sunday. On Sunday I would get up early and hitch-hike the long distance from that town over to the coast and to Pacifica and my comfortable church settings. Almost instantly I realized that things were not the same anymore with the ones I had spent so much of my time with. There seemed to be a disconnected feeling that I was not able to get a handle on. This, in turn, left me with a kind of emptiness as I attended the Sunday morning worship meetings.

After church services, when everyone was heading home, I made my usual small talk. Secretly I was hoping someone would invite me to their home for dinner, and then I headed back to the job house and the people who were now my life. As soon as I got back there and walked into the house I sensed such emptiness within that place.

I soon came up with a plan to change the house and to re-create their environment to match the one I had when I lived with the Christian family. So from that position I began walking through the house like a missionary on a mission of change. My thinking was, "Lord, thank you for giving me this work to do, now you just go off and tend to other things and I will fix these people up good and proper, you just watch and wait, I have it all under control. Oh, by the way Lord, if I need anything I will call ok." Does that sound familiar to anyone? In our determination to change people do we set off on our own campaigns trying to make others shape up? We run "helter-skelter" over others trying to bring change, but all for the wrong reasons. Well, this is what I engaged in and the Lord gave me just enough "rope" to allow me to go to the end of its length. The truth is I reached the end of that particular rope fairly quickly.

I knew exactly what changes needed immediate attention in order to re-create the house operations best suited to fit my own world. I announced that from now on I wanted us to have dinner with everyone in attendance at the table. There was no longer to be any chaos in the kitchen, but things were to be conducted as a family from now on. I looked upon "day one" of my creation as "being good." We sat around the table like little bumps on a log and of course, with me in charge of each bump. This was great, yet I was only getting started on this project.

Next, in order of creation were bible studies. From now on we would be meeting in the assigned area, (I needed to find one) on Wednesday evening from seven to eight. This was also good and I looked upon this ruling as "day two" in the creative steps in the plan of God as I engaged in bringing order out of chaos. I was really on a "roll!"

After those first two "creative steps" I then tried to usher in the third; however from that point things went sour real fast. I had been there now for almost two months and each day brought more unsettling thoughts that my time there was winding down. This really bothered me and I kept dismissing such thoughts as from Satan.

I still had not seen anyone get "saved" yet and this too was disappointing to me. However, putting step three into gear was going to solve all my problems and usher me into realms of unbelievable advantages and respect. Finally the big day arrived for me to put "day three" into operation. This was going to be the day of days!

I had stumbled upon a teaching that said that I could claim anything and it would happen providing I really, by faith, believed hard enough and struggled against all opposing realities in order to see whatever I was asking for to materialize. This teaching opened up whole new realms of possibilities and I could not wait to apply what I had learned, of course using Laird as my "victim." So I was good to go and I told Laird that God was going to completely heal him and in a few minutes he would no longer be confined to a wheel chair. I asked him if he was prepared for such unlimited use of his new walking abilities and he looked at me with a non-expressive gaze. I took that to mean he was ok with it, so I wheeled him into the privacy of his bedroom as I wanted no unbelievers in there at a time such as this. I then went on to explain to him the importance of the following two biblical passages.

"Is any among you sick? Let him call for the elders of the church; and let them pray over him, anointing him with oil in the name of the Lord: and the prayer of faith shall save him that is sick, and the Lord shall raise him up; and if he have committed sins, it shall be forgiven him." (James 14-15)

"But let him ask in faith, nothing doubting: for he that doubteth is like the surge of the sea driven by the wind and tossed." (James 1:6)

Once I had thoroughly indoctrinated him into the importance of having faith and not doubting, I then told him it was time to pray. I was so happy; this was going to be my big day into the world of full time healing evangelism. So I laid my hands firmly upon the top of his head, and shutting my eyes tight, I began to pray like never before. I prayed and prayed and prayed and with each commanding statement I shook his head with my hands as a way of bringing finality to each thing that I shouted out in faith. During this intense time I heard Lard call my name which broke the spirit of my praying. I opened my eyes and saw that during my vigorous excitement and total oblivion to my surroundings, I had managed to literally push him almost out of the chair. I had shaken his head with each announcement of healing and restoration brought on by the force of my hands pushing down upon him. Finally, right before he hit the floor, he called out and so ended the prayer. The poor kid lost his healing; his faith just was not strong enough to allow me to push him out of the chair. The healing was waiting on the floor; I was sorry his faith wavered. So ended my creative ways and I also went on to lose my job. This was a crushing blow to me for I was so discouraged and felt like a total fool. Can you believe it? I did not even get a chance to fulfil the other creation steps. What a bummer!

It was on a Saturday afternoon and I was told I needed to leave the next day. One can only guess as to how I felt, not only in front of these people, but also before the Lord. Shame and embarrassment held me tight in its grip owing to wounded pride and now, owing to the loss of the job, my self worth was in jeopardy.

Chapter Seventeen

A Hearing Faith

Before I continue with the order of events I need to inject this particular and valuable lesson I learned, not only at the time I had in praying for Laird to be healed, but also other future situations. This message was branded upon me through lessons that were taught in some very painful ways.

Please note the important common factor concerning faith and prayer. When I attempted to pray for Laird I did so without being personally prompted by the Holy Spirit. The prayer I launched out on was all about me and for my own agenda. One might ask the question whether this means that we are not to pray for anyone unless we are told so by the Lord. As I see it one can pray for people all they want, however there is only one type of prayer that is effective and brings results. It is that kind of praying that we should exalt as we pray for others. Here is a half portion of scripture to apply in what I am saying here:

"And the prayer of faith shall save the sick," (James 5:15)

The key ingredient here is "the prayer of faith." In the church today the most misunderstood aspect is faith and prayer. It is completely misinterpreted and abused in some of the most unimaginable ways.

There was a time when I prayed for Laird's grandmother who was sick. It was the complete opposite to the prayer in which I engaged with Laird. One day, as I passed by her bedroom door I could hear that she was suffering with a serious cough. In the process of coughing she called out to God for help. Instantly the Lord impressed upon my spirit to pray for her. This impression to pray for her instantly troubled my heart and I now had a burden which compelled me forward. With Laird, I had no such thing; it would have been better if I had!

After a few moments of bringing my will into submission before the Lord I finally approached this lady and told her I would like to pray for her. She consented so together we bowed our heads and I said a nice "churchy" type of prayer. The kind of prayer said on a given Sunday morning in modern churches today. I then left the room, yet the burden to pray for her had not left me. Then the Lord spoke, quite directly and made known to me His will. "Go back in there and pray for her this time with the laying on of hands!" Wow, I was supercharged by this Word and with that instruction I now had all the right stuff to pray the "prayer of faith" for I had heard the "Word of God." This is the common ingredient and is so missed or ignored in many churches today, and needs to be addressed immediately.

Once more I entered into her room and let her know we needed to pray again. This time I instructed her as to how I would carry out this prayer, by the laying on of hands as the Bible said. Upon hearing me say this she instantly refused this type of praying, for her church taught against it. Once she said this to me, the burden to pray left and I was now released from praying. It is a shame for I knew in the Spirit that the Lord was going to heal her, but owing to a teaching she had turned aside the grace of God in wanting to heal her. I left the room and she continued to cough and live in a religious form.

"So then faith cometh by hearing, and hearing by the word of God," (Romans 10:17)

Three portions in this sentence of truth need to be both analysed and developed. They are: "faith," "hearing" and "hearing by the word of God." Any and all faith we have, whether big or small comes to us via hearing and that hearing is by the word of God. Too often within Christian communications and speech we toss words and phrases around like basket balls. Sometimes they miss the loop and go bouncing down court. In order for us to communicate effectively we need to use words and meaning of words to "hit target."

Our faith or lack of faith swings on this fact and that is our ability in hearing.

We can say we have faith and tell others to "have faith" or "keep the faith" (whatever that means) until the cows come home, yet still be empty and void of spiritual realities. It is interesting to note that in the New Testament gospels Jesus spoke of faith in two extremes. They were, "great faith" and "little faith." If we can somehow make a connection here with faith and see that its foundation is built upon the "word of God" then to increase our faith we can give ear to "hearing" and that is the bottom line here. When we get into trouble it is when we make so called "statements of faith" which do not come from the word of God spoken to us but from our own "wishful thinking."

"For I say, through the grace given unto me, to every man that is among you, not to think of himself more highly than he ought to think; but to think soberly, according as God hath dealt to every man the measure of faith." (Romans 12:3)

The preceding verse and those that follow are one train of thought and should not be taken out of context. However, the reality is that each man has been dealt a measure of faith. With that in mind we then can know that within us is a measure of faith. What we do with it is determined by our will. That in itself is a whole other message. I personally think this "measure of faith" is worked out within all of us throughout the course of our lives. When we are in dangerous situations who do we turn to for help? The measure of faith causes us to call out to God. That is just the way it is.

"Now faith is the substance of things hoped for, the evidence of things not seen." (Hebrews 11:1)

Substance: (the real or essential part or element of anything; essence, reality or basic matter.) Evidence: (something that tends to prove; ground for belief) Now we have two words defined and let's try to get a feel for this text as we digest it. Faith is the substance of things hoped for. Well the Word of God is the substance of our hopes, dreams and aspirations. Without it we are incomplete and "not connected!" The evidence follows on the heels of our faith which grows under constant "hearing" of the "Word of God." With that said, let's move on here and try to tie this all together in such a way as to get the correct meaning of this "faith issue."

Sad, but true, some ministers and groups have spun off the faith thing and literally perverted it to manipulate for monetary gain. It sickens me to see this type of gospel being advocated on prime time television. Leaders of these movements have become as bold as to make faith a tool of "get rich" by swaying others to give in order to be blessed. But notice here the "giving" is to them so they can benefit. They ride off the faith of others all the while encouraging us to have "seed faith." So, be that as it is, we need to see how true faith can be applied in a working way in our daily lives.

"But without faith it is impossible to please him: for he that cometh to God must believe that he is, and that he is a rewarder of them that diligently seek him." (Hebrews 11:6).

No one can decide the existence of God for us, each of us

as individuals needs to make that determination on our own. I can testify at this time that within my life I now have the knowledge that God exists because he lives within my heart. Furthermore, it is in my best interest to live for Him. With the introduction to "Hearing Faith" presented lets look at what it means to be active in hearing faith.

"Verily, verily, I say unto you, He that entereth not by the door into the sheepfold, but climbeth up some other way, the same is a thief and a robber. But he that entereth in by the door is the shepherd of the sheep. To him the porter openeth; and the sheep hear his voice: and he calleth his own sheep by name, and leadeth them out. And when he putteth forth his own sheep, he goeth before them, and the sheep follow him: for they know his voice. And a stranger will they not follow, but will flee from him: for they know not the voice of strangers." (John 10:1-5)

How do we hear in order to have faith? Firstly, not everything we hear is the word of God. Thieves and robbers will constantly invade our space trying to speak things other than that which comes from the Good Shepherd. Our ears need to be knowledgeable in this area of our lives. We hear so much nowadays, but ask this. Is that which I am hearing producing faith in me or does it breed confusion and doubt? So then, how can I really know if God is speaking to me? How can I really know God's voice in my hearing?

We recognize God's voice by his calling us by name. This speaks to me that in order for Him to call us by name that he must know us in such a way that we know His voice. We come to know His voice by way of communication which includes our own patterns of speech. In other words he uses the way we talk and the way we say things as the means to speak to us.

All the times that I have heard the Lord have been times when the word spoken to me was in easy to recognize speech patterns. The way I speak to others and the way I communicate from day to day is also the way the Lord speaks to me. This is very effective and always causes me to instantly know the voice of the Lord. The speech pattern by which God reveals Himself to me is sent to me in my own style of words and is 100% right on target. Therefore, I recognize the Lord for He speaks to me in the same way as I speak. This same way applies to each of us in this matter and is so simple yet so profound.

Now that we know that "faith comes to us by hearing and hearing by the word of God" we need to hear the word in order to know how to proceed. Too many mistakes are made when we attempt to move on a particular course in the hope that God will speak something to us before we reach the end. Many wasted days and dead-end missions result from the notion of "blind faith." Nowhere in the bible is there any such thing as walking without first of all receiving some kind of commandment walk. To be walking or traveling one must not do so in blind faith. In order to make spiritual progress we need to learn this important truth. We must get the Lord to speak to us in order for us to have faith to put into motion the project we are being directed in. "When in doubt over what to do, pray until the word comes through."

Too often we try to move the hand of God by stepping out into some idea and trying to get God to bless it. We call it a move of faith, but deep down inside we know it is only a desperate attempt to move out of our own situation and create another one. It would be nice if we could act on our own ideas and do things for God out of the imaginations of the heart, but in God's program of promises we have to wait until He gives us walking instructions. The waiting is hard, but the way of the Lord for each of us is to stay planted where we are until we receive word otherwise. Below is a true story of faith and word combination.

I was working on a job in Idaho. It was a farm labor job and I was a ranch hand. The work was hard and the hours were long. The job was ok, but the politics of the job were insane. On several occasions I considered leaving and going else-where, but never did so. By this time in my life I had learned the lesson not to move out ahead of the Lord. One day, I ran across a job opportunity which I applied for, but never really took it as being anything serious.

One morning when I awoke to get ready for another working day I was sick, so I called in sick on that particular day. The phone rang later on that morning and it was the people to whom I had sent the application. They were asking me to come down to Oregon to talk to them. This news really surprised me for I had completely forgotten about them. Without even thinking I told them I would be there on Monday morning. As soon as I hung up the phone it hit me as to what I had just done.

My daughter was there and I asked her what she thought I should do. We had a heart-to-heart talk in the living room regarding my current work and this new job. She told me to go and pray about it because she could see my distress. I went into the bedroom and got down on my knees before the Lord. When I got up I remember having a calm peace which was an indicator of His will for me to go. At that time I had not been given a word, but only His peace. I was interpreting the peace as His blessing on going.

Now here was the hard part, I had to walk over to my boss and tell him I needed Monday off. So I devised a plan, like something the Old Testament Abraham did on different occasions. I asked for the rest of the week off owing to a family matter that had arisen in Oregon. How is that for a misleading, yet truthful statement? I figured I could keep my job here just in case the other one did not work out. However, my boss had the nerve to ask me straight out why I was going to Oregon. I could not think of any thing to tell him other than the real truth and that I was looking for another job; upon telling him that I was fired.

As you can imagine, when I got back to the house I was ready to pray again.

The prayer began like this, "Lord what you have done to me now? I had a good thing going here even though I did not like some things, yet I was willing to stay. Now Lord, I am fired and I have nothing." I then got up off my knees and went and called the people in Oregon to try to get a guarantee of work. As it turned out it was only a job interview and nothing more. Well that is not what I needed to hear.

I headed back to my prayer time. "Lord how could you do this to me? I had a job here and now I have nothing. My life is over and I am now in serious trouble and you don't even care." I prayed along those lines, and then the Lord spoke peace to my troubled heart. "You go to Oregon I am in this move." I returned conversation by asking the Lord. "Will I get the job? Will you give me some definite facts I can go on?" He responded back "No I wont, you will just have to trust me." I received the word spoken and I heard the word of God and I now had the faith I needed to travel on.

When we are in a tight situation and we are up against the wall, who do we turn to when we need answers? God will answer us in the realm of His word to us and we then receive the faith needed to make the journey onward. We can apply His word as we hear it and let that word carry us on in faith. Trust is merely a keeping agent as we go forth in faith which comes by hearing and hearing by the word of God.

Chapter Eighteen

My Prayer Closet

"Let us therefore come boldly unto the throne of
grace that we may obtain mercy, and find grace
to help in time of need." (Hebrews 4:16)

Not only did I lose my job with Laird, but I also
lost my bed and my source of food. I was completely hit from all three sides. This was another
pressure point for me and I needed to head to my prayer
closet just as fast as I could go. I had a place up on the hillside from this house that was hidden in the forest. It had a
small open meadow which was a perfect place for me to
spend time in prayer. In times past I used this place for a
time of out-pouring to the Lord and "knocking loudly" upon
the "Throne of Grace." It was there that I had many serious
talks with the Lord during which time I said things to Him
that came from deep within my soul. This place of prayer
was like a "shipping and receiving station." I shipped out my
prayers through wrapped packages of raw needs. The Lord
received them and mailed back to me huge freights of peace

and a strong sense of His nearness. At times I literally thought He was going to appear before my very eyes.

I was there once more and I must have stayed there for well over an hour. I did a great deal of confessing of the errors of my ways. I did some complaining over my situation and I also laid out my needs before the Lord and told Him how lost I was in this whole mess.

Some might consider this type of one-to-one praying to be a little extreme and unprincipled; however, "desperate times require desperate measures." Under those conditions I talked to the Lord and by the time I left the hillside I knew once more that everything was going to be fine. I had such a joy of anticipation over what lay ahead and what the Lord was going to do for me. I knew that everything was under control, as promised in the verse, "And we know that all things work together for good to them that love God, to them who are called according to His purpose." (Romans 8:28) This verse became my source of encouragement, especially when I came to places that seemed hard in my life. This verse spoke volumes to my heart. I took it to mean that those things that at times can discourage and bring us down, are tools used in the Lord's work within us to bring us along as we travel under His purposes for us. This was such a mind boggling concept and when I attempted to grasp the entire scope of such truth it was almost more than I could comprehend.

I came down from the hill with a trouble free spirit. I knew the situation was under the control of God's keeping ability and I was still His child. The Lord was not going to toss me in the junk yard, but rather I was merely in a process of steps of His working within my life. I returned to the house for my final night. While there I instructed Laird not to feel bad about firing me for the Lord had me in His program and I was moving into another realm in His plan for my life.

I had learned much while at this particular home and when I left I departed with a depth of knowledge that transformed my life. This, once again, enlarged the foundational settings under my feet. Everything that was happening to me was all part of the Lord's work in my life to reshape and transform by using events and situations to bring me to places of brokenness and surrender.

I had learned something of interest and value from each member of that family. Laird, for example, brought me into his world of the disabled and broken in body. Yet, in spite of this outward display of human body there was a person inside who was no different than I. We talked on things and shared ideas, interests, hopes and dreams. I learned that the handicapped did not want to be thought of as second class citizens, but rather they wanted to be treated normally as real people in life. I got the healing I needed while I worked in this job. The Lord was in control and I shall never forget Laird.

I also learned about prayer and the difference between effective praying and shallow praying. I brought my needs to the Lord and sought Him in my times of distress and He always came through just when I thought I could not carry on any longer. There is no right way or wrong way in praying when we enter into a one-to-one relationship with the Lord. The beauty of knowing Jesus is to have the freedom to express to Him the very thoughts and intents of the heart. Approaching the Lord in the fear that we might say or do the wrong thing can cripple us by doing nothing and saying nothing. This results in a broken communication between the Lord and us. This only hurts the heart of God for in our fear we hold back from what could otherwise be a rich and fulfilling walk that can only be known by our complete trust in Him.

The next day I got up and gathered my few belongings and left the house. Once more another chapter had been finalized and a new one was right around the corner. My whole life seemed to be geared towards this type of movement. At times I could not see the hand of the Lord in what was happening, however, my trust in Him got me through.

Chapter Nineteen

Places

"And Jacob awaked out of his sleep, and he said, Surely the Lord is in this place; and I knew it not." (Genesis 28:16)

I left early the following morning. It was Sunday and I needed to get to church which meant hitch-hiking the long distance. The Lord provided me with the rides I needed and soon I was sitting in the congregation. The preaching message was anointed and the worship brought to my soul such a wonderful presence of the Lord. I had not told anyone of my situation for I wanted the Lord to reveal to me what-ever it was He wanted. This was just the way I operated in my trusting department. I went through the entire service and still had nothing from the Lord. During this time I have to admit that I battled with the turmoil brought on by the power of human understanding conflicting against waiting on the Lord.

The service slowly came to an end and people were now heading home. I was really bordering on panic at this point for I was indeed between a "rock and a hard place." I had no idea what I was going to do if I walked out of the service without a clear and concise direction.

I walked slowly past two brothers who were talking on the steps of the church. The conversation I overheard between them really caught my attention. I overheard Ed saying that they planned on opening the house ministry. However, Paul would be the only one there with him. Another person was needed, but so far the Lord had not revealed who that person would be

I knew that this was the day of my new beginnings. The Lord came through again for me and not a moment too soon. I was almost at the point of despair over what appeared to be a lack of intervention on His part. Truthfully speaking, I had laid it all on the line before the Lord concerning this situation. Furthermore, I had no other plans of operation that I could put into play just in case things did not work out with God. Too often we make deals with the Lord using this method. We come to a deadlock before Him concerning a need of extreme importance. Yet, we hold back on total reliance upon the Lord's ability to see us through to the finishing point. We hold in reserve a few of our own plans just in case God's way does not work or, for that matter, does not meet our standards. Then, if He does not come through or is silent in the times we claim to need him, we accuse Him of not being there for us. Since God sees the heart and is not given over to playing our games, He remains off-center until we finally come to terms with really wanting Him without any deals on our part.

Upon hearing those two brothers speaking I had that all too familiar quickening of my spirit. It was no accident that I just happened to overhear them speaking. The Spirit of God took their words and sent them, like a sharp arrow, deep inside my spirit. Upon hearing this conversation and having the statement made by Ed was all the revelation I needed in order to understand the plan of God for me at that time.

I approached Ed and we talked concerning what the Lord had confirmed to me just then. It did catch him off-guard and I remember that he seemed to be wavering over the timing of me moving in. I told him this, "Ed the Lord wants me to be at the house in this ministry." I admonished him to put aside his own ideas and be obedient to the Lord. Upon hearing this he did the only thing any obedient child of God could do, he accepted the truth as the Lord spoke to him through me.

We can be bold when the Lord speaks to us concerning a particular thing. Once we know His voice, (hearing faith), we can then move out in boldness and confidence in the direction pointed out to us. If others seem to be a little hesitant in such matters, then it becomes just a matter of us educating them in what we know to be of the Lord. The Spirit of God takes our words and confirms them to the appropriate parties in order to settle any confusion or doubt.

I went on to enter into this type of house ministry which was not like the house I lived in during my earlier days. It was a big house and had a huge monthly mortgage. All three of us brothers attended the same church fellowship. The house itself was connected to the church organization yet it was up to Ed, Paul and I to make the monthly house payments. This was a shock to my world and was a wake-up call to a whole new learning process, for in order for me to make monthly payments I had to work. The word "work" was not in my vocabulary. I had worked for Laird, but that was different compared to that which was being demanded of me this time.

There was no getting out of it. I had a part to play in this ministry and now my new song was taking on new lyrics along these notes. "Send me the money Lord, deliver me from work, and please hear my prayer!" The Lord sent me the money alright, but it came by way of physical sweat and blood. My world of being spiritual and dynamic was now history. Instead I held a shovel in my hand and got blisters on my feet.

The house ministry we had formed was targeted for juvenile kids who were in trouble with the law. On the weekends we would drive down to the local correction center and take whoever wanted to come with us back to the house. We shared Jesus with these kids and fruit was bearing as the Holy Spirit worked in their hearts. I saw some of them come to the Lord and begin to change and grow.

During the week, we got up each morning and after morning private prayers we all gathered in the front room for a time of team prayers and sharing. I have to admit I did not really like being there for most of the time I did not care for the team I was surrounded with.

This was a time of growth once again for me, for I now had to learn how to get along with fellow Christians and how to deal with faults and shortcomings. I can assure you that these two brothers had faults and major rough edges. My present imperfect condition was tested many times over by having to be patient with Ed and Paul. However, as time went on they slowly "began to improve" and I was relieved to see that happen.

I stayed there for a time then once more I moved on to other areas of growth brought on by change and more change. The Lord was constantly doing new work in me and each step I took built larger foundations under my life to stand on. I now had a "new song" to sing, but I was a long way from singing this song in perfect harmony.

As that "fly picture" I described earlier I was now ready to fly off the launching pad of my recovery table. For the most part, the foundation had been pretty much laid within my life. I had been tested and re-tested and now the building itself was ready to begin. I made my all important decision to commit plus dedicate my entire life to Christ. I have never once regretted doing so! I praise God that He chose me out of the world and took the time to heal me and restore life back in me. Now it was time to spread my wings and once more head into the "promised land" that the Lord showed me. This was my land to conquer and dwell in. I was more than ready to hit the road and not fail as I did in times past.

Had it not been for "Calvary" I would not be here today. My story does not end here, but merely begins. I packed my bags and left on the Lord's highway. I have no regrets, but I do have sorrows, not from choosing the Lord, but from the life He called me to walk in.

I left the house ministry on good terms and with the blessing of the brothers. Ed went on to marry and he too started his life in that department. Paul stayed in his home town and I never saw him again. I went back to my home town carrying with me the life changing message that had been "forged and branded upon my soul."

A note of sadness besides, both David and my spiritual mom died after I left. David died of cancer. He was not even twenty-five years old. He left a young mother and son behind, but is now in heaven and I am sure he is having fun.

Some time later, "mom" died too. She had a stroke and the Lord took her home. All doors to my spiritual home-land were now closed forever. I was totally on my own. Now it was just Jesus and me.

In memory to both of those two pillars of impact upon my life I now sing my song of gratitude and service to the Lord. It is my desire to give back what I have gleaned from the things both mom and David taught me during the course of their lives. Mom always told me this, "The Lord has a very real work for you to do, and I will always uphold you tenderly before His throne and pray that you will always do his will joyfully, Amen!" I was barely twenty when I arrived there and stayed until I was twenty three.

Chapter Twenty

Hitch-Hiking God's Way

"And, behold, I am with thee, and will keep thee in all places whither thou goest, and will bring thee again into this land; for I will not leave thee, until I have done that which I have spoken to thee of." (Genesis 28:15)

The Lord gave me this verse the night before I was leaving Pacifica. This was such a blessing to me for I needed a promise from God to carry with me as I traveled homeward. Hitch-hiking can be dangerous and that which lies ahead is unknown, but now I had a promise to carry with me. As a result I had the added strength to go forward in the confidence of His word to me.

Since I had been with the Lord and traveled by hitch-hiking, I had some awesome experiences and strange situations unfold. On one occasion, I was heading to Oakland out of San Francisco. I had begun to see that the Lord was using this time of taking rides as a tool for me to witness to others and I did so willingly most of the time. There were times though when I was not so willing to share.

Two homosexuals gave me a ride in their convertible. It was a sunny afternoon, the top was down and I climbed into the back seat. Soon we were on the bay bridge and suddenly I felt the presence of the Lord very strongly. His words started to enter into my spirit and I became certain that He wanted me to speak the words He had given me to these two people. However, I fought against doing this for I had entered into judgment and disdain over what type of people they happened to be. Therefore, I held my tongue and fought against speaking out for Jesus. As I said, we were on the bay bridge heading to Oakland. As usual there was a great deal of traffic and the noise made it impossible to talk to them, unless I wanted to shout at them. So I said to the Lord, "I can't talk to them for they cannot hear me above the noise of the traffic and commotion." The driver of the car was extremely weird and he was making even more noise than the traffic outside. This enabled me to further justify not speaking the words within me. What happened next was awesome.

The words inside temporarily subsided and I was free of the prompting to speak. What a relief that was! I also thought that I had got one over on the Lord this time by presenting to Him a problem that He could not handle. Boy was I ever mistaken!

I sat peaceful and happy as the traffic was moving, but without warning the traffic on the entire upper bridge suddenly slowed down and came to a complete stop. I could not believe this was happening at a time like this. All I wanted to do was to get to the next town, but God had His agenda too and I needed to adjust mine in accordance with His. The words came back into my heart again with more force than before. I was bursting at the seams and needed to speak His words in order to be free of the pressure upon me. The Lord then told me, "Ok, now you can talk for I have stopped the traffic."

It became quite clear to me that unless I spoke to them that we were not going to go anywhere. Each word within me came out one by one and as I spoke I sensed a release from the pressure within me. The neat thing about it was that His word was not falling on deaf ears, but was going out with power and anointing. From what I could tell the passenger was receiving these words and God was dealing with Him. On the other hand, the driver was reacting by attempting to drown out what was being said by yelling and shouting like a mad man. As soon as everything that was bottled up within was spoken then my job was finished and immediately the traffic started moving once more. Once again, I learned another lesson of God teaching me truth and justice in the Spirit.

First of all, I need to be willing and obedient to His words inside me. I cannot hold back from telling others what He gives me to say. I also must put aside my own fears and personal agenda when the Lord shows up to talk to someone. His timing is perfect and we are not to get in the way of what He is doing in someone's life because we "don't have the time." After all, when all is said and done, what are we here on this earth to do anyway!?

Chapter Twenty-One

Hitch-Hiking
to God

And though thy beginning was small, Yet thy latter end would greatly increase. (Job 8:7)

God had truly been good and given His grace to me even though I never once deserved it. I have learned a great deal over the past twenty-five years and not all of it has been easy. However, each step of the way the Lord revealed His love and grace.

The above verse was one the Lord gave me personally and it speaks of small beginnings and increase in latter times. My beginning was as small as one can imagine. I came to the Lord as I was and not a moment too soon as at that time I only had the clothes on my back and empty pockets. He took my small beginning and built upon it and brought me where I am today.

I went on to get my high school diploma. I entered the work force and learned to be productive. I married and raised a family, obtained a driver's license and maintained a car and insurance, etc. Perhaps in the eyes of some these things are "small potatoes, "but for me they were tremendous victories.

I have learned that there is a difference between the Body of Christ and organized church doctrinal institutions. God commands us to be in submission to authority and to obey the Lord as He speaks to us that which He desires from us as His children. My hitch-hiking days came to a close as I began to change and take on a more responsible way of life. Change is not something we need to fear, but is there for us to be transformed. Many times I saw things that made me feel as if it was out of my reach to achieve. Marriage, for example, seemed to be for others, yet not for me. However, when my foundations began to expand under my feet then confidence took root within my life and heart.

There were some in the body of Christ who had been crippled by the life they lived while in the world. Change for them seemed impossible and they appeared to have no incentive to move on beyond what they had become even though they were saved. I, for one, had to be careful over the ill feelings of disgust I sometimes held towards them over this for I was determined not to give up and I accepted whatever conditions existed in my life. Instead I turned to Jesus as my lord and sought Him for change and pleaded for Him to heal me of any and all things that kept me from life with Him.

There are issues that surround us that will not just go away by our ignoring them. It is only when we face issues and take responsibility over our own actions, radically seeking the Lord for change that we can ever hope to see our lives in the plan God has for us.

If anyone were to ask me which was the most important thing I would tell others it would be to not play games with God and waste your life spinning in circles going nowhere.

Be strong in the Lord and in the power of His might. Tap into what He has for you and do not take a back seat to Satan and his lies. As a child of God you can have victories and live in the Promised Land that exists within the relationship between you and Jesus. Discover the gifts and the talents God has given you and apply them in your life and live for God.

The title of this book, Hitch-Hiking to God, is unusual, but is real for each of us. For in a more real and practical way all of us are hitch-hiking to God in one way or another. In that definition we are all on the same highway standing there with thumbs out and waiting.

Biography

Born in Spokane, Washington, William Leaf lived there until the age of eighteen. He spent a short time in Ca. where he walked and talked with God on the beaches there. This was where he made his first steps of growth in God.

He is married and now lives in Coos Bay, Oregon.

He enjoys the coast, spending as much spare time walking the sandy beaches as his life allows. The beach is where William feels the closest to God.

He has enjoyed fishing and loves being out on the ocean catching deep sea fish.

It has been his desire to fulfil God's calling in his life by using the gift of writing that God has given him as a means of bringing glory to God's name.

Printed in the United States
1197800001B/235-690

Got Porn?

A Christian Man's Guide to Personal Freedom

Dr. Kirk Austin

CONTENTS

ACKNOWLEDGMENTS

To dad - for modelling a lifetime of compassion,
integrity and wisdom.

Men wanted for hazardous journey. Small wages, long months of complete darkness, constant danger, safe return doubtful. Honor and recognition in case of success. – Earnest Shackleton

Endurance

The year was 1914 and Earnest Shackleton was recruiting for an upcoming expedition and was looking for a rare type of man - one with strength and grit and a quest for adventure. While most of us would merely scoff at the opportunity and breeze past the posting, Shackleton was successful in his campaign eventually recruiting 28 hardy men.

Shackleton's goal was ambitious. Setting sail, he would make his way to the Antarctic by way of the Weddell Sea, south of Argentina. Once there, he and his men would cross the polar cap by dog sled team. As a seasoned veteran to long expeditions Shackleton knew that the adventure ahead would be difficult. But he remained optimistic about their success. Little did he know at the outset, that this journey would become one of the greatest stories of survival of the 20th Century's nautical history.

The ship was christened the '*Endurance*' after Shackleton's family motto "by endurance we conquer". This was a modern ship by the day's standard. A three-masted, wooden schooner, the vessel was equipped for polar expedition with a coal burning steam engine to ensure that it would make headway regardless of environmental conditions. However, in a cryptic twist of irony, her name would serve as a portent of things to come. The men were about to embark on a journey of drama and danger that would take them through the next two years of their lives.

Beginning in Fall of 1914, the ship and men set sail pressing toward the South Pole. As circumstances would dictate, pack ice impaired their progress and by mid-January the Endurance was completely stopped by thickening slurry. Despite attempts by the crew to free her, the Endurance became entombed by polar ice. For the next 11 months she would remain frozen, the crew persevering against biting winds and subarctic temperatures.

In late October of 1915, the ice began to shift and compress. Knowing that the ship was doomed, Shackleton abandoned his ship after removing what provisions could be salvaged. On November 21, 1915, the Endurance surrendered to the relentless pressure of the crushing ice and sank.

Of the supplies that were salvaged, three small wooden rescue boats were among them. These would later prove to be essential to their very survival. For all intents and purposes, the crew and ship were lost at sea. They had not made contact since their departure, and the world was a lifetime away. For his part, Shackleton called their giant iceberg 'Patience Camp' and pressed on making the best of his circumstances. This would be their home for another five months.

Over the following months the ice had been breaking up into smaller flows. The space on which "Patience Camp" was situated was becoming more dangerous as it could indiscriminately break apart, separating the crew and supplies. Knowing that time was short, Shackleton planned a daring escape. With no time to spare, he loaded the three small boats with men and supplies and set sail toward a tiny island 100 miles into the open ocean and arrived at their destination five days later. Elephant Island was a small piece of frozen rock that was home to the ocean mammals in its area. This would be the first time the men had stood on solid ground in almost 500 days.

Shackleton knew that despite their victory, it would be brief. To the outside world, the Endurance and crew had perished. No one was coming to rescue them. He also realized that with the rations that they had, and the sea animals that they could catch, their time for survival was limited. He had one idea; a long-shot plan for survival with impossible odds, yet it was his only hope. The island of South Georgia was 800 miles away. On it was a whaling station with enough supplies and resources to bring salvation to the trapped men. Selecting his best crew members he boarded a small life boat and set sail.

To say that his goal was ambitious is a laughable understatement. Having only a sextant as a navigation tool, Shackleton would survey the stars in order to set his direction. However, given the intemperate seas and inclement skies this was no simple enterprise. Miscalculation would mean missing their destination by hundreds of miles and the death of all members of his crew. He had to be exact. There was no margin for error.

Setting sail, they encountered rough seas. This was not the playful surf of a destination vacation. These were angry and blistering seas. The water itself would freeze to their small craft, weighing it down. As their boat gained weight, it would sink lower to the water line. Swirling sea water would rush into their boat, threatening to sink all aboard. For their part, the men would climb onto the craft and chip away at the ice to free it from its captivity. The waves were enormous and any misstep could mean certain death. They would also bail sea water from the boat without ceasing. To make matters worse, sextant readings required that one man would need to stand on the boat to gain sight of the stars, at the height of enormous sea swells. Two others held his legs for balance and support; all the while the boat would be reeling from the turbulent surf. All aboard were soaked through and through by the pounding breakers.

They were freezing, chafed and frostbitten by the subarctic temperature and blistering winds. Sleep was infrequent and broken. Yet after 14 days on the unrelenting sea, they realized their goal and arrived at the island of South Georgia.

There was one problem. Gaining the advantage of the island, they had arrived on the wrong side. And given sea conditions, their boat was no longer safe to continue the journey around the island to the whaling station on the other side. Again Shackleton made a daring wager - they would cross the island on foot. Between their position and the whaling station however, were mountains and glacial ranges. With the resources available, the men took screws from their sailing craft and mounted them through the soles of their boots, making a crude type of crampon for traction on the ice.

Beginning their journey with a small piece of rope and sparse provisions, they began. Braving the elements they climbed mountains, navigated glacial precipices and hidden crevasses. Taking little time for rest and nourishment the men pressed onward toward their goal. Thirty six hours later the crew arrived at the whaling station to the utter amazement of all whom they encountered.

Organizing the resources needed to rescue the men would take another several months. Weather and pack ice made three attempts at rescue unsuccessful. However, in late August 1916 Shackleton arrived back at Elephant Island and rescued the remainder of his crew. No one perished. They had endured two years of captivity in one of the most inhospitable environments on the planet. It was truly a miracle.

The Question

Screen writers couldn't script a better choreographed tale of danger. This was edge-of-your-seat drama housed in harsh and bitter circumstances. These weren't Hollywood actors who could retire to their leisure trailers after an eight hour film shoot. These were real men, living day after freezing day in one of the most uninviting settings on the earth. And yet, in the end, they all had somehow summoned the will to endure the test.

My question is this: What would it take for a person to survive under such difficult circumstances?

Let's be clear - God hadn't made a different sort of man for this trial. These were not comic book heroes, capable of super-human feats of strength and endurance. These were fathers and sons and brothers. And they were ordinary. So what would it take to survive?

Above all, I believe that faith would be indispensable. First, the collective faith of the team would be of great help in buoying their morale. Encouraging each other to press on and not lose hope could lift the spirits of those in need of an emotional boost. But more than this, a personal faith in a God that could bring salvation would be the fervent hope of every man. This faith would be gut level, raw and vital. This faith would anchor deep and genuine prayer. And their faithful trust in God and anticipation that they would someday see their loved ones again would, in the words of Jeremiah, call them forward to a hope and a future.

I believe that trust would also be an essential ingredient to survival. First, a person would need to trust their Captain. Under such circumstances, most wouldn't put blind faith in just anyone. His reputation and embodied authority would command a sense of trust - that he knew what he was doing and where he was going.

In addition, a person would also need to trust their fraternity with their very lives. Knowing that every man was responsible, and doing their part, would promote the assurance that they were all doing what they could to survive and make it home. Likewise, a person would have to play their part in extending trustworthiness to others. Acceptance of personal responsibility would mean that even the person himself would pull their weight, and do what they could humanly do to sustain the lives of others.

Surviving vs. Thriving

Trust is hard for a lot of men.

Ask an average guy to participate in a relevant work project and most will be happy to lend their effort. Ask a man to share his emotions with you and your request will be met with a measure of hesitancy. For many men, trust takes time; it must be nurtured.

For the most part, our culture teaches men to be self-reliant, autonomous and strong. Images of the independent, self-determined and macho men fill popular media. Most men want their sons to grow up tough. Given the option of putting their sons in figure skating or hockey, most guys want their boys to chase a puck, not learn to triple axel. Given the option of putting their boys in ballet or football, most men would want their sons on the smash-mouth grid iron, not the dance floor. The rules of engagement are "Don't be weak", "Don't be vulnerable" and "Don't be too emotional".

This sentiment has influenced the nature of men's relationships within the church. Most men are content to show up on Sunday with the family and "do" church. Some may even be happy to contribute to the voluntary activities that occur within the church community; a small group, kids programming, or a meal delivery program perhaps. But ask a man "Who knows your soul?", or "Who really knows you, at the core of your being?" and most men will give you a blank stare or start squirming.

The reality is that when I ask this question of men I work with, their answer is "no one". Most men don't give genuine access of heart-related matters to anyone else. Most men don't have a Jonathan / David type of relationship with another man; a guy who knows the stuff they're working through, accepts them anyway, and keeps calling them toward Jesus. And this creates problems.

Men need other men. While it is possible for men to remain independent and rugged within the church, what often occurs is isolation rather than connection. They opt for solitary survival. And when the storms of life hit, they have little recourse than to baton down the hatches and remain in solitude out in the bitter cold.

Thriving is qualitatively different than surviving. It requires that men actively co-labor with God and each other. It means that men are fully engaged, not disconnected. It is men who are plugged into a real relationship with their God. It is men who are genuinely committed to their own growth and maturity in their faith. It is men who practically care for their families and communities. And it is men that cheer one another along in their journey of faith. Vibrant community requires that men are fully engaged.

Here is where the conversation is relevant. The topics of pornography and men's sexual purity are delicate to begin with. Try to start a conversation with a man on sexuality or his relationship to pornography, and most men will redirect the topic. And where men are entangled with the explicit medium, they often withdraw from the conversation completely. Specifically, they withdraw from their active role in Christian community. They pull away from relationships, isolate from activities, and often struggle in secret, and through their solitude the church suffers for it. What they need most is for other men to enter their story and to paraphrase Galatians 6:1, gently restore them, calling them out of their captivity without becoming entangled themselves.

What's needed is for men to recognize that they have a particular place in calling their brothers out of captivity to pornography. When one falls, others need to be there to pick them up. Men need to know that their story won't be ridiculed & that they won't be shamed. These merely promote hidden-ness. Instead, men who are stuck need to know that there is a way out of their captivity to pornography; and that they can be met with grace, forgiveness and restoration.

It is with this in mind that the following material was developed. It frames the delicate discussion about the nature of pornography, the nature of captivity and asks each man to honestly evaluate his relationship with the medium. And while there are many men that don't struggle with explicit material, there are many more that are struggling in secret and silence and don't know how to get free.

What they need most is for their Godly fraternity to enter their story and call them into the identity and relationship with the One who can set and keep them free.

2

The Problem

When there's an elephant in the room, introduce him.
– Randy Pausch

Brenda & David

The first few minutes of our counseling session were quite friendly, polite and even benign. Brenda and David were a good looking couple in their mid-forties. Their sun-kissed tans and blond hair hinted at their active lifestyles. Both were well dressed in business attire as they had coordinated a mutual time to meet at the end of their work day.

Brenda was an energetic and articulate woman that had retained her youthful figure despite having several children. Her career as an urban professional kept her schedule busy, but she made sure that she had the time for her growing children and husband. David was a lawyer with a thriving practice. Long hours and a hectic calendar kept him extremely busy. But, despite the frenetic schedule, he made sure to make the time for his kids' soccer and volleyball schedules.

On first pass, I thought that the topic of our first session would be one of distance in their relationship, or a need for better communication skills, or a pesky issue that wouldn't go away. But emerging from the calm of our introduction, Brenda's anger flashed across her face as she slammed her fist against the table and heatedly asked - "What the hell are these?"

Brenda was referring to the handful of pictures that she had printed off of their home computer's archive of recent internet searches. The pictures were explicit in nature, containing images of nude women and of people engaging in various sex-related acts.

Her gaze was unrelenting and her jaw clenched as she searched his face for an answer. Pain was etched on her expression, and her hands were shaking as she impelled him to look at their content. To my surprise, David looked relieved - someone finally knew.

In the time that followed, David was fairly candid about his growing appetite and pursuit of pornography. Of course he was reluctant to divulge the extent and details of what he had been looking at. It was too shameful, too embarrassing and too painful. And yet he was relieved that he was finally able to get his problem into the light. He was held captive to his lust for pornography and his habitual pattern of secrecy. Now at least there was a chance that he could get free.

Pastoral Story

The story of Brenda and David isn't exclusive to the counselor's office. It is a phenomenon that is occurring with more frequency in the pastor's office, during prayer at men's groups and over coffee with close friends. And for every man who is deciding to voice his struggle with pornography, there are many more who remain silent and suffer in secret.

Perhaps it is the shame and guilt, especially within the Church, of acknowledging their struggle that holds some men in their silence and secrecy. Perhaps it's the stigma. Perhaps it is the lack of knowledge of the resources that are available to them that paralyzes men into non-action. Or perhaps it's the lack of conversation within the Christian community about sexuality and it's discipleship that keeps it limited to specialist conferences, hushed conversations, or a professional's office.

Within my clinical counselling practice I have been noticing an interesting trend in recent years. Though I may begin my counselling sessions with couples discussing their mutual marital difficulties, when pressed, many of the men admit to using pornography as part of their private activities - their wives don't know, or have recently found out. And many of them haven't made the connection between their porn use and the marital problems that they currently face.

In recent years I have also had conversations with pastors, other counselors, and denominational church leaders. Their message is the same. Within their congregations, their seminaries and their pulpits, pornography use is at an epidemic level. In 2004, Promise Keepers reported that 50% of men attending their conferences struggled with pornography. I would argue that with the pace and integration of technology, and the generation that is growing up with it, that this percentage is significantly under-reported and rapidly increasing.

One pastor that I recently spoke with offered a sobering statistic. Over coffee one afternoon, he mentioned that at a marriage conference that their church had coordinated, they had asked attendees to complete a confidential questionnaire at the onset of their weekend. To his surprise, the majority of the men attending the conference admitted to struggling with pornography use. What was more surprising was that the nature of survey also revealed that they had not disclosed their struggle to their wives or others. They were struggling in solitude, keeping their shame and guilt to themselves. They were stuck in their secrecy. Though this may be an isolated event, it is my opinion that it may reflect a wider phenomenon.

Talk to any pastor or counseling professional and they will tell you that any positive change toward personal freedom requires that an individual open their story to others. Hidden-ness merely masks the pain and struggle. Time doesn't heal all wounds, it just creates chronological distance from the real issues. Change requires that the struggle is brought out of the darkness and into the light. It needs to be opened to trusted others, and the One who can bring freedom. An essential component to change is that the individual is *ready* to do the work.

READINESS

Since the material within this book is intended to be practical in nature it is important to have a quick discussion about the concept of **readiness**. In order to get the most out of the ideas within the material you will need to become active. Rather than passively reading the book as a list of ideas, it is important not only to comprehend and reflect on the contents, but to 'try on' some of the exercises. However, like most people the notion of merely jumping in can seem a bit daunting.

Whether tip toeing into the pool or doing a cannon ball is your nature, it is most important that you are in a state of readiness. By being ready, you gain the most value from the pages that follow.

Jim

Jim found himself becoming increasingly frustrated in recent months. Occasionally his emotion would pour out on the colleagues around him through his dirty looks, sarcasm, or the muttering he would speak in tones so low that people couldn't quite make out his words. But more than this, he knew his frustration through the knot in the pit of his stomach and the tension headaches that he would medicate on a daily basis. No matter how hard he would try to 'manage' his feelings, they would leak out.

The first to address Jim's behavior was his personal assistant. Lynn had worked with Jim for several years and was a recipient of his tempestuous emotions. He hadn't always been this way, but in recent months Jim appeared to be more moody and brooding.

"Is everything okay, Jim?' Lynn asked one morning.

'Yeah...everything is fine' he said, moving past her question to his to-do list. Despite Lynn's genuine concern and repeated efforts to help in the weeks that followed she was met with the same reply- 'I'm fine thanks'.

Over the months that followed, Jim's performance as one of the company's top producers became lack luster. This drew the attention of the company's General Manager. Opening up to his boss's inquiries, Jim began to disclose the parts of his life that were sinking below the water line. He expressed a general frustration with his work, that his marriage was tanking and that he was bothered by the general state of his life. As a result, Jim was referred to see me, to see if I could help with his situation.

The difficulty became apparent in our first meeting. Jim began by launching into a long-winded diatribe about how everything was *her* fault. The *'her'* in this equation was his wife. According to Jim, *'she didn't do this...or she always did that'*. And all of the difficulties at work were the result of all that s*he* had been doing.

Upon my probing, Jim indicated that he had a long-standing relationship with pornography that had taken on a more prominent role in recent months. And during our conversation, he was quite candid about the nature of his porn use. He was spending time looking at increasingly more explicit and hard-core material on a daily basis. But he claimed that it actually helped him to de-stress. And besides, he reasoned, his porn use was a direct result of *her* actions or inactions. "If she was more affectionate...", "If she initiated more sex..." If she was less critical..." He argued that he wouldn't need to use pornography if *she* were different. "Besides", he reasoned, "it wasn't hurting anyone".

Though I gave Jim the elbow room to vent during the first session, it became a game of psychological dodge-ball when I turned the questions toward him. Questions of his involvement, behavior and participation in the relational difficulties were avoided or turned back on her. Discussion of potential strategies, resources, books and ideas were frequently truncated before they were fully developed - *'why would he need these if she was the one who needed to do the work?'*

And when I asked them to meet with me as a couple, Jim would repeatedly interrupt his wife 'mid-sentence' and deny her the opportunity to finish her ideas. Sadly, Jim ended the counseling sessions after just a few weeks, claiming that they were a waste of time.

Like most counselors, I hate to see individuals quit the counseling relationship before they realize its potential value; personal insight, strategies, resources and positive change. The reality is that despite the efforts of even the best counselors, there are times when their work doesn't have the desired outcome. Many times this is because the rate of change in the individual is dependent on their level of psychological readiness. In Jim's case, he just wasn't *ready* to do the work.

Positive change requires *readiness* - a psychological state in which a person is positioned to take action. Like a baseball player waiting for the pitch, or a tennis player beginning to serve, each needs to be 'ready' mentally, emotionally and physically in order to execute to the best of their ability. In Jim's case, he was simply not ready to fully engage the counseling process.

HOPE

Personal readiness means that an individual is motivated to take an in-depth inventory of their life, and are prepared to strategize and take action toward the future that they desire. There are several elements to personal readiness that can be summarized in the acronym *HOPE*. They are as follows:

- **Honesty**

The element of honesty relates to the intent of the individual to seek the unvarnished truth; to see things as they really are. Regardless of how the individual might feel to hear hard information, they nevertheless seek it out, knowing that it will produce good fruit. Generally, honesty is aimed inward. Individuals who are psychologically ready are willing to look at their actions, emotions, motivations and history. Further, they are honest in their evaluation of the consequences of each of these on the others in their lives. They are honest with themselves.

Similarly, honesty is also directed outwards, towards others. Individuals who are psychologically ready are willing to be transparent regarding their emotions, motivations, personal behavior and subsequent consequences. In this way, honesty maintains a form of genuine communication with others. Moreover, individuals who are honest are willing to 'speak the truth in love' to those around them.

In the seminal work that I did with Jim, it became apparent that he was unwilling to be honest either with himself or with those around him. When prompted by those who cared about him, he would provide a patent 'I'm fine' in order to avoid being genuine about his frustration. And when probed about the nature of his frustration or porn use, he would provide only character attacks on his wife, or redirect the focus away from himself. In this way he remained stuck through his unwillingness to be honest with himself and others.

- **Openness**

The element of openness relates to the intent of the individual to refrain from closing themselves off from truth, influence, ideas, vision and strategies. In general, individuals who are psychologically ready are in a state of open-mindedness - they are receptive. This is not to say that they are accepting of every new idea that comes along. Rather, they are willing to hear, explore and examine the content that others are putting before them.

Generally, individuals who are psychologically ready are open to hear what others have to say. They are open to hearing the truth. They are open to others' influence and guidance. They are open to new ideas and resources. They are open to dream and envision a positive change. And they are open to strategizing toward their preferred outcome. By way of contrast, individuals who are not psychologically ready remain guarded, resistant and closed to the same.

During the brief time that I worked with Jim, it became apparent that he was unwilling to remain open to the process of counseling. From the outset, he was guarded, reluctant and resistant. He was closed to the suggestion that he played any part in his level of frustration or of having a part in creating his own level of happiness. Jim was closed to ideas that were outside of his perception of the situation. And he was closed to exploring the resources and strategies that were being presented for his benefit. In this way, Jim's lack of openness stunted his readiness to fully participate in evaluating and envisioning a positive outcome.

- ## Permission

The element of permission relates to the intent of the individual to consent to try new things. Where openness reflects an individual's intent to consider new ideas and strategies, permission goes one step further in that it corresponds to a person's intent to try them. Permission allows movement.

Change requires action. Action can be daunting, hard and exhausting. Individuals who are psychologically ready are willing to permit themselves to try new things. They permit themselves to risk - regardless of how their feelings or fear may challenge them. They permit themselves to fail, knowing that failure can help them to grow. They permit themselves to change, regardless of the emotional or social difficulty that might follow.

Jim was unwilling to permit change. Since he had locked his sites on his wife as the perpetrator of his unhappiness, he was convinced that he had little work to do. Rather, he was the one that required change; in his outlook, motives and actions. In this way, he froze the process of change through his lack of permission to try new things.

- ## Expectation of Positive Outcomes

The element of expectation relates to the intent of the individual to anticipate positive outcomes. Whereas permission relates to an individual's consenting to try new ideas and strategies, few people would consent to execute these actions if they thought that there was no benefit. Individuals who are psychologically ready generally believe that positive change is worth pursuing and is attainable. Further, they expect that beneficial results will occur in the long run.

Again, Jim truncated the counseling relationship early in its formative process. In doing so, he was convinced that pressing further was a fruitless activity. In his mind, the origin of his frustration was outside of himself and that the steps necessary for change were clearly his wife's responsibility. And since the counseling process wasn't fast-tracking his agenda, he held little optimism for its success.

All for One and One for All.

I remember as a kid, playing the three musketeers. Looking back, I am sure that our game was most likely prompted by an after school TV special. But to small children, our sword play was just as animated and choreographed as a summer blockbuster - and no stunt doubles were needed. We would swashbuckle our invisible foe with twig in hand, and swagger about our back yards. And when we had conquered our imaginary enemy we would join our swords and unite in our reverie 'all for one and one for all'. Of course in the next hour we would be hitting baseballs, collecting bugs or running in a dozen different directions that our hyperactive bodies would carry us. However, at the time our call meant that we were unified and singular.

In the same way, psychological readiness requires *all of its parts* make a unified and singular entity. Honesty, openness, permission and expecting positive outcomes, as elements of readiness are all necessary to promote positive movement. And positive movement is limited without all of the elements in play.

Consider an individual who is captive to their pornography use. Despite knowing that they need to make some changes to promote greater freedom, they do not know where to start - so they come to you for advice. Like most people who would want to help, you begin by asking questions to clarify the nature, extent and context of their issues.

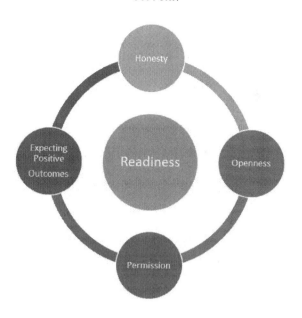

However, if when you ask questions about the nature of their porn use habits, they 'forget' to tell you about the stash of illicit magazines that they have hidden in their house, it would become apparent how their lack of honesty can hamper your work. Regardless of whether the dishonesty is motivated by denial, ego, or personal blind-spots, the individual's readiness to change is hampered.

Now imagine that this same individual finally admits to hiding their porn stash. By way of personal honesty, this is a good thing. However, psychological readiness would still be incomplete if the person was not open to the ideas and strategies you may suggest. If you hear, 'I've already tried that and it doesn't work', or, 'No way- I am not doing *that*!' when you suggest an accountability partner or a porn blocker for their computer, your efforts to help will be significantly minimized. Only when the individual adopts a position of openness, in concert with honesty, can your help be of any good. Without it, the individual voluntarily closes off the possibility and strategies for change.

This same individual, when committing to be honest (with you and themselves) and open (to your ideas and strategies) faces another hurdle: permission. Whereas honesty and openness hold the promise of positive movement, they are inert without permission. This same individual may plan and strategize to be accountable or load protective software. But, unless they permit themselves to face their fear of looking weak to others, and actually preemptively disclose when they are tempted, they will stay stuck. In essence it is "ready, aim…aim…aim" - without the fire. Individuals' who won't permit themselves to risk new ventures or the specter of failure truncate the process of positive change.

Lastly, people who hold low expectations for the change process, merely tolerate the change process, but never fully experience the value of the practice. For example, the individual who has committed to block pornography from their home computer will have diminished tenacity to complete the process if they believe that it really won't work. Their lack of positive expectation will rob them of the energy to sustain their efforts. Or as another example, an individual may struggle to contact a peer during a time of temptation. However, if their expectations remain positive (that their efforts will promote freedom), they will remain committed to their plan despite their struggle. In this way, all of the elements are necessary and essential for psychological readiness to promote maximum value.

As it relates to this material

With the readiness model in mind, individuals who will gain the most from the ideas within these pages will maintain a position of honesty and openness with themselves and others. And they will give themselves permission to try new things and will expect that positive outcomes will be the fruit of their effort.

Regarding the contents of this book:

Honesty will open up the possibility of positive change and greater freedom.

- It means you have to take a fearless and in-depth inventory of what's working and what isn't working in your life.

- It doesn't mean that you run around telling everyone about what's going on in your life. It means that you have a select few individuals that are committed to you and your spiritual growth.

Openness to new ideas will uncover resources and pathways to positive change.

- It doesn't mean you have to accept or execute every idea - just hear them out. You can weigh the ideas against your resources, time and energy.

Permission to try new things will create momentum toward positive change.

- It means that you give yourself permission to risk, to do hard things, to fall on your face, to get back up, to dust yourself off, and to learn and grow from your experiences.

- It means pressing through your fears.

Expectation of positive outcomes means that you are hoping for the best and are compelled to keep moving toward positive change.

- It is not vain fantasy or rose colored glasses.

- It is a form of positive realism; a settledness - that your hard work will provide a positive dividend.

Note: As you come to the end of this section reflect on how ready you have been to deal with some of the pornographic content that you struggle with. Now consider the following questionnaire and complete it. Remember honesty is an essential ingredient to freedom.

Readiness Questionnaire

Instructions: Regarding your pornography use, rate yourself on the following questions.

	High	Medium			Low
1. How honest have I been with my significant others?	5	4	3	2	1
2. How honest have I been with my friends?	5	4	3	2	1
3. How honest have I been with myself?	5	4	3	2	1
4. How open am I to others advice?	5	4	3	2	1
5. How open am I to be accountable with others?	5	4	3	2	1
6. How open am I to using computer porn blockers?	5	4	3	2	1
7. How open am I to call someone *before* I slip?	5	4	3	2	1
8. How open am I to dealing with what got me here?	5	4	3	2	1
9. How prepared am I to try something new?	5	4	3	2	1
10. How prepared am I to be vulnerable?	5	4	3	2	1
11. How prepared am I to do my homework?	5	4	3	2	1
12. What is the likelihood that I will stop porn use?	5	4	3	2	1
13. What is the likelihood that all of my effort will pay off?	5	4	3	2	1

Questions to consider.

1.   For questions that you answered medium to low - what are some of the reasons that you think you rated them so low?

_____

_____

_____

_____

_____

_____

_____

_____

_____

_____

_____

2.   For questions that you answered medium to low - what would it take to rate them higher on the scale?

_____

_____

_____

_____

_____

_____

_____

_____

_____

_____

_____

3

The Nature of the Industry

What pornography is really about, ultimately, isn't sex but death.

- Susan Sontag

Road Trip

When was the first time you looked at pornography?

Of course, I am making a generalized assumption that you have, in fact, seen pornographic material at some point in your life. Perhaps your first time was an accident; an inadvertent glance at illicit material on television or in a magazine. There is also a chance that you sought it out and found it; a cluster of boys circling around a porno-mag that one student brought to school. I was in grade 6.

For the first 13 years of my life I lived in central Canada - in particular, the prairie provinces of Saskatchewan and Manitoba. And like every young boy in my generation, we grew up with skates on our feet and hockey sticks in our hands. During the winter months, ice was freely available on every frozen pond and outdoor rink. Playing organized hockey was a rite of passage, and a yearly tournament to a neighboring city or province was the highlight of the year's schedule.

The memory of my first exposure to pornography was during a long-distance hockey tournament. Having to take a day long bus ride, my best friend and I hatched a plan to occupy our time during the long hours on the road. Slinking into a local corner store we searched out a magazine that, in our opinion, was racy and titillating. In reality, it was a comic book with cartoon boobies and buttocks. But to us it was the real deal.

In order to circumvent the scrutiny of the parental bus-chaperones, we cleverly swapped the cover of a hockey magazine for the cover of our prized porno-mag. We were sure that we were in the clear and that our plan was bulletproof. But, as the bus droned through the miles and we thumbed through our prize, one of the coaches walked by and stopped at our seat section. Perhaps it was our giggling, or the guilty looks on our faces that tipped him off, but the coach knew that something was up. Asking to see the magazine, we handed it forward and froze.

To our horror, he started laughing and then held it up to the parents on the bus and announced sarcastically - "The boys are doing a bit of hockey research". And then, he turned and walked away. The trip carried on as if nothing had happened. No consequences, no morality-talk, no debriefing, just good natured smiles and pats on the back from the men on board.

It's interesting that this is my first memory of pornography. I couldn't have been more than 11 or 12 at the time, and there was no moral compass guiding my choices, telling me this was wrong. At the time, my family wasn't even slightly religious, and the opposite sex was a normal part of my peer interest. And yet this memory still registers as significant enough to occupy mental space.

What is interesting about my story is that it is similar to so many others. In men's groups that I have facilitated in the past few years, early childhood exposure to pornography seems to be the norm. In fact, research shows that the average age of children's first time exposure is 11 (Internet Filter Review, 2006). Even by today's standards, that is barely pubescent. What's more, 90% of kids between the ages of 8 to 16 have seen pornographic content. And of youth between 15 to 17 years old, 80% have watched hard-core pornography. These statistics, though disturbing, make intuitive sense given the nature of the porn industry.

Porn's Success

If you think about it, certain aspects of the nature of pornography have allowed it to infiltrate so deeply into our current culture. In particular, porn has gained significant traction because of it's cost, availability, secrecy and cultural acceptance. It is because of these features that porn creates a toxic attachment to many men. These themes provide a useful framework to discuss the nature of the industry.

- **Cost**

When I was an adolescent preparing for my hockey trip, the only place that pornography was available was the corner store. This was the norm. The majority of illicit content that was widely available came in the form of paper. Magazine racks were the main conduit of the tempting medium. The game changed with the advent and accessibility of technology.

With technology came a rapid transition in the medium and nature of illicit pornographic content. In 2009, the Canadian documentary *Porndemic* surveyed the nature of the porn industry worldwide. Their synopsis was that the porn industry is one of the fastest growing global industries. Gone are the days and market share of the paper based porno-mags. They are rapidly being made obsolete by tech driven replacements.

The worldwide appetite for titillating material remains a constant. As long as people have sex drives there will be a hunger for pornography. However, technology allows the global consumer an unending range of content to choose from. Still photos are giving way to moving images. And we're not talking about big budget feature films with porn stars and movie sets. Though these still exist, and claim a portion of the erotic market place, they have to share the market with low budget amateur fare. According to

Porndemic, one of the fastest growing segments of the industry are films shot with amateurs and posted on the internet. Production value is not the point, access to market is.

In fact, the fastest growing web sites of illicit material give access to their content for free. *Free!* By attracting a volume of viewers, they are able to data mine their viewing audience, tracking types of keywords and sexual-preference searches from their website. Money can be made as point of purchase, by up-selling their audience to click through sites or banner ads. Like the local drug dealer peddling to a kiddie-school, they give it away, knowing that they are fueling an appetite. People will be back for more.

- **Availability**

Do you remember your first cell phone? As a young family therapist working for the Salvation Army, I was given a portable phone to remain connected to my head office as I travelled around our city. However, compared to the thin elegant and powerful phones of today, my cell phone in the early 1990s was the size of a Kleenex box or brick. Perhaps in the day, the phone was state of the art. But by today's standards it is a relic that has more use as a door stop than a cell phone. Advances in technology are realizing Bill Gates' vision that there will be computers in every school, home and office. What's more, almost every young person has a computer in their backpack and a cell phone in their pocket. Devices are fully integrated; web-enabled for real time texting, phone conversations, appointment management and internet surfing.

This advancement and proliferation of technology has meant that people have access to illicit content anywhere at any time, if they have access to a computer or cell phone. In 2006, the Internet Filter Review indicated that approximately 25% of all internet searches are for pornography. In 2008, Patrick Carnes, a leading expert on sex addiction, added to that statistic suggesting that approximately 8% of daily emails contain pornographic content.

In 2010, a Washington D.C. think tank, Pew Research Center, noted that 3 out of 4 youth between the ages of 12-17 years of age have a personal cell phone. According to researchers, that number represents a 30% increase in youth cell phone users *since* Promise Keepers conducted their survey in 2004. And given the nature of integrated technology, the proliferation of internet hot-spots, and web search traffic, the average youth has access to illicit content 24/7. Renowned psychologist Phillip Zimbardo estimates that by the time a typical youth graduates high school, he may have spent approximately 10,000 hours gaming or surfing pornography.

This type of web traffic-potential provides a lucrative business opportunity for companies wanting to cash in on porn's gold rush. Wendy and Larry Maltz, in their book *The Porn Trap* (2008) commented that since the opportunity for consumer business is growing so rapidly, so does the promise of potential revenue. As a result, national telecom and media giants are entering the market. It is estimated that annual worldwide revenues could exceed 300 Billion dollars (Carnes, 2008), and that cell phone access alone could yield over 2 Billion dollars in annual revenue. And given the borderless nature of the internet, this trend only expands the accessibility of the industry to an interested public. Recent advances in 3D technology and person-to-person visual connectivity only promise to push these numbers higher.

- **Secrecy**

Let's face it, most men don't like to be vulnerable. They don't like to be exposed, or perceived as weak. It's too scary, too raw, and too uncomfortable. And to admit that he is a regular consumer of pornography makes a man feel as though he is a pariah or a sleaze. This is true for men who struggle within the Christian community, or whether they are non-churched regular community members. Research shows that of those individuals accessing illicit material online, approximately 70% hide it from others (Maltz, 2008).

This is where the internet provides an interesting opportunity. Back in the day, a man would have to walk into a corner store to access print-oriented pornographic materials. This meant that he would have to summon the courage to face any residual shame or guilt that were prompted by his conscience. And if he was successful in locating a preferred porno-mag, he would have to look the store keeper in the eyes as he paid for the material. Someone else would know.

This all changed with the proliferation of technology. Since paper has given way to pixels, anyone can access any image in the privacy of their own home, or office, or cell phone. And behind closed doors, this provides the individual with a sense of anonymity; there is no looking anyone in the eyes at a cash register. There is the illusion of security and that no one will ever know. And given this anonymity, it creates the illusion that there are no consequences.

I use the word *illusion* purposefully. Just because no one else sees the actual use of porn doesn't mean that it is anonymous or victimless. Whether the consequences are alienation from others, distance from one's spouse, loss of personal integrity, loss of employment, or merely guilt and shame, porn use has very real consequences. It is the lack of awareness of them that provides the allure of the medium.

• **Cultural Acceptance**

I remember that as a kid we had a black and white TV. Old staples like Saturday morning cartoons, Gilligan's Island and the Brady Bunch were the standard fare of our TV consumption. These were the days where the sultriest behaviour by women was the breathy tones of Ginger or the pigtails of Mary-Anne. And the bedroom behaviour of Mr. And Mrs. Brady was confined to late night discussions about work or the kids. Anything racier was considered pornographic for young viewers.

Those days are long gone. Back in the day, pornographic material was easy to identify. Today, explicit images blend into the fabric of our everyday lives. Lingerie companies send magazines to our door steps and purchase prime time real estate on network television for their 'special programming'. TV commercials, music videos and lyrics, movies of the week and even video games have blurred the lines of what's acceptable, or at least tolerated. Culture has become saturated, and clean lines are harder to find. Where at one point in time, a person had to go out of their way to find porn, now they have to go out of their way to avoid it.

- **Attachment**

The term pornography essentially refers to images or writings about prostitutes. However, in our 21st Century culture, men are confronted with images that don't cleanly fit into this category, but may still be alluring. In their book *The Porn Trap* (2008), Wendy & Larry Maltz offer a useful definition of pornography. In their opinion pornography is *"any sexually explicit material that is intended to be or is used as a sexual outlet."*

What I like about their definition is that it isn't anchored to a specific subject matter. Material such as hard core videos or magazines would clearly fit into the definition. Yet other material that is innocuous to some men may be pornographic for others. For instance, shoe advertisements may be used for sexual purposes for men with a shoe fetish or common store catalogues may be off limits to men who find the female bra sections too much to handle. And yet for the vast majority of men, shoe catalogues or women's underwear flyers pose no moral dilemma at all.

Maltz's definition of pornography not only frames the type of material that may be pornographic but it also includes the *type of relationship* that a person has with the material. In psychological terms, their definition includes the idea of the type of *attachment* that the individual has with a subject matter.

Some men that I have worked with have demonstrated a clearly *attached* relationship to porn. They see nothing wrong with illicit material and include it in their lives as something that they do in their free time. To be fair, many of these men do not hold a Judeo-Christian world view and their choices are driven by their sexual appetites. Others may have a moral objection to pornographic content but have a clear attachment to it. In their case, they are captive to their urges and impulses that compel them to pursue it.

Within an attachment framework, others that I have met with have demonstrated an *avoidant* relationship to porn. For these men, clearly-defined moral boundaries and the ability to live by those boundaries keep them clear of sexualized material. For some, there is no compelling draw or gravitational pull towards engaging explicit material. For these men there is just no appeal. Others have built safeguards into their lives. Accountable relationships, computer filters, and other protections mean that they are able to successfully avoid pornographic content.

However, it has been my counselling experience that an increasing number of Christian men have an *ambivalent* attachment to porn. That is, they are drawn to and may participate in explicit material, and then strongly avoid it. Some men that I have worked with have mentioned that they dabble in sexualized content, only to feel repulsed by it later on. Some access porn on an occasional basis through purposeful internet searches, only to later avoid it for a season.

With the ambivalent type of attachment, there is a push-pull dynamic in effect. Like Paul in Romans 7, the thing that most men don't want to do they eventually do. And once they obtain it, they feel guilt, shame and remorse, they repent, and then strongly move away from it for a period of time. This lasts for a brief period, and then they feel enticed once again.

UNSAFE

The Maltz's definition of pornography leaves a lot of room for men's individual differences. Some men will relate to pornographic content in attached or avoidant ways while others relate to it in ambivalent ways. In the same way, men will find some content innocuous, and other content titillating. Knowing whether content is problematic or pornographic to a man's particular interests can be difficult given the subjective nature of individual taste or particular content. Having a simple guide can help to discern what type of material can be problematic.

There is a simple model that I use with men to help them identify the type of material that is inappropriate for them. It is a sort of litmus test; a guide to determine if the content that they are looking at or thinking about is appropriate and acceptable. I use the acronym UNSAFE to frame the model: Unhealthy, Negative emotions, Secret, Alienating, Fantasy-based, and Excuses.

The idea that something is *unhealthy* refers to whether negative consequences would occur if the person consumes the material in question. For example, sexualized content has a way of invading a person's thought life, even after it is no longer physically present. If the content in question produces residual sexual images that invade ones thought life, or remains as images for sexual fantasy, the content is most likely off limits. Additionally, if the content produces unhealthy elevated sexual expectations, it is most likely inappropriate. And if the content would be damaging to your relationships if others found out, or if there would be negative consequences of some kind, the content in question is ill advised.

Another characteristic to evaluate questionable content is if the material produces *negative emotions.* Emotions such as guilt, shame and remorse frequently follow the use of pornography. And prolonged use of explicit material often produces the emotion of depression. These types of emotions similarly follow content that a person finds sexually titillating. Such emotions serve as a clue that the content may be ill-advised.

If a material is consumed in *secret*, or a person hides their activity from others, the activity may be illegitimate. Looking at content in question, in private, usually means that a person has a *check* in their spirit to begin with. Hiding it usually means that they don't want others to know what they are looking at. These are clues that the content may be objectionable to you or significant others around you.

If the activity or medium produces relational distance and *alienation* from others, it is most likely ill-advised. Often, if a person has a growing difficulty with pornography, they begin to withdraw from key relationships. Emotional distance, being closed off, and relational detachment are clues that a person may have a problem. If alienation is the result of viewing content in question, it is most likely not ok.

If the material in question is non-real, it may be a problem. For example, much of the professional porn industry relies on actors playing particular roles. These are real people playing out unreal scenarios. Content that may be used sexually, that originates from unreal sources or storylines is most likely problematic. Following this line of thinking, fantasy is unreal. It is different from memory, in that fantasy hasn't happened. If content is sexual in nature, occupies mental space, or if time is spent in *fantasizing* about the material, it may be a problem.

Lastly, if a person has to make *excuses* to justify their activity the content is likely to be in question. When held up to other people's scrutiny, if questions remain about the content's legitimacy, most people would cease their activity. However, if a person continues despite others objections or if they have to rationalize their viewing habits, the content may be illegitimate.

The questions and prompts on the following page more fully delineate how to use the model. It can be used to assess the acceptability of content that you or others are looking at. It can also be used as a test of sorts to clarify if viewed content is suitable for the individual looking at it.

UNSAFE Questionnaire

Unhealthy

- ☐ Is it damaging to your relationships?
- ☐ If someone found out, would there be negative consequences?
- ☐ Does it create unhealthy mental images?
- ☐ Does it create unhealthy sexual expectations?

Negative Emotions

- ☐ Does it produce guilt?
- ☐ Does it produce shame?
- ☐ Does it produce depression?
- ☐ Does it produce a sense of emptiness?

Secret

- ☐ Is it done is private?
- ☐ Do you make sure that no one is around when you do it?
- ☐ Do you hide it?
- ☐ Do you take steps to cover it up?

Alienating

- ☐ Does it make you withdraw from others?
- ☐ Does it make you close yourself off?
- ☐ Do you create emotional distance?
- ☐ Do you refrain from being fully known?

Fantasy-Based

- ☐ Is it based on people you don't know?
- ☐ Is it based on fantasy storylines?
- ☐ Does it consume your mental and emotional energy?
- ☐ Do you continue to recall the images at a later time?

Excuses

- ☐ Do you defend it to others?
- ☐ Do you make excuses to yourself about it?
- ☐ Do you minimize it to yourself or others?

4

The General Nature of Captivity

In a consumer society there are two kinds of slaves. The prisoners
of addiction and the prisoners of envy. - Ivan Ilich

Proverbs 7

Dear friend, do what I tell you; treasure my careful instructions.
Do what I say and you'll live well. My teaching is as precious as
your eyesight — guard it! Write it out on the back of your hands;
etch it on the chambers of your heart. Talk to Wisdom as to a
sister. Treat Insight as your companion. They'll be with you to fend
off the Temptress — that smooth-talking, honey-tongued
Seductress.

As I stood at the window of my house looking out through the
shutters, watching the mindless crowd stroll by, I spotted a young
man without any sense. Arriving at the corner of the street where
she lived, then turning up the path to her house. It was dusk, the
evening coming on, the darkness thickening into night. Just then, a
woman met him — she'd been **lying in wait** for him, **dressed to
seduce him**.

Brazen and brash she was, restless and roaming, never at home,
walking the streets, loitering in the mall, hanging out at every
corner in town. She threw her arms around him and kissed him,
boldly took his arm and said, "I've got all the makings for a feast
— today I made my offerings, my vows are all paid, So now I've
come to find you,   hoping to catch sight of your face — and here
you are! I've spread fresh, clean sheets on my bed,   **colorful
imported** linens. My bed is **aromatic with spices** and **exotic
fragrances**.   Come,   let's   make   **love   all   night**,

spend the night in **ecstatic lovemaking**! My husband's not home; **he's away on business**, and he won't be back for a month." Soon she has him eating out of her hand, bewitched by her honeyed speech. Before you know it, he's trotting behind her, like a calf led to the butcher shop, like a stag lured into ambush and then shot with an arrow, like a bird flying into a net not knowing that its flying **life is over**.

So, friends, listen to me, take these words of mine most seriously. Don't fool around with a woman like that; don't even stroll through her neighborhood. **Countless victims come under her spell**; she's the **death** of many a poor man. She runs a halfway house to hell, fits you out with a shroud and a coffin.
- *The Message*

What I like about Proverbs 7 is its easy segue with the medium of pornography and the process of captivity. As discussed earlier, explicit material is growing in volume, content and variety by the day. It's on every virtual street corner in America. And for every Christian man, it whispers for his attention, hoping to seduce him. She promises ecstasy; whatever your fantasy; whatever your preference or interest; whatever ignites your lust - it's there for you. Just reach out and take it and it will satisfy your thirst. This is the pitch and the promise.

James 1:14 is useful here. "*But your own evil longings tempt you. They lead you on and drag you away. When they are allowed to grow, they give birth to sin. When sin has grown up, it gives birth to death.*" The power of the medium is that it pitches to your God-given human nature and sex drive. Let's be honest, men like the idea of sex. The problem is that lust takes your normal God-given desire for sex and twists it toward the illegitimate.

In his book *Wired for Intimacy* (2010), William Struthers discusses the typical porn-search process. In particular, a man can surf for pornographic material with little physiological impact. However, when he happens to come across material that fits his unique arousal template there is an immediate and significant spike in his neurochemicals. Lust is inflamed, and there is no turning back.

Proverbs 7 goes on in parallel with the nature of the porn industry promising anonymity. In whispered tones she tries to seduce, and in whispered tones she convinces him of the secrecy of their rendezvous. "No one will know..." she offers, giving illegitimate permission for his compliance. Freely he follows, engaging his will, submitting to her offer. And before long he is held captive, and in captivity, he dies.

Bill

A few years ago I counselled a Christian man in his mid-40's. Bill was a long and slim man whose medium build was hidden beneath his plaid work shirts and blue jeans. His face was weathered and hands were calloused from the physical work that he performed day after day. He was seeing me because his wife had given him an ultimatum - "See a counsellor about your porn use or I tell the pastor".

Over the weeks that followed, we explored the nature of his pornography use. Sexually active as a young man, he had experimented with several partners. His peer group actively engaged pornographic material, giving him access and tacit permission. When he met his wife-to-be, he rationalized that he was done with his former way of life, and that he would be exclusive with his wife. However, since their marriage, the whispers of the temptress continued to call to him. The next few years were a blend of periods of pornography use, followed by confession to his wife, followed by periods of freedom. His wife finally had enough of his ambivalent dance with pornography, when she could predict the content of his message when he said

"We need to talk". He needed more help than she could give.

As it turned out in my discussions with Bill, his wife had seen only the tip of the iceberg. The more Bill disclosed about his porn use, the deeper, layered and more complex were the issues related to it. Following the *death* symbolism of Proverbs 7 we performed a psychological autopsy on the nature of his porn use.

As a means of creating awareness of Bill's idiosyncratic relationship with porn, we explored the how's, what's and when's of his habit. To his surprise, there was a pattern to his porn use.

Often, he would be triggered toward porn use through increases in his stress levels or corresponding emotions. Work, arguments, and even the buildup of little things acted as triggers as they accumulated over time. And when he would use illicit material, he would surf for particular sex acts that catered to his appetite.

When he was finished, he would meticulously wipe the computer of any evidence or trail of what he had looked at. He would feel bad for a period of time, but eventually go back for more a few weeks later. This was the typical pattern of the captive dance he had with the temptress.

Unfortunately, Bill's story isn't one of great success. Remember the idea of readiness? Bill wasn't fully ready to change. During our time together, he gained tremendous insight into the emotions, rationalizations, triggers and precursors that patterned his porn use. And when it came to putting a plan in place to arrest his pornography use, he was fully engaged in strategizing. However, it became clear over time that he wouldn't follow through with his plan is any sustained fashion. It was apparent that Bill was captive to his porn use.

The Captivity Process

It is useful to understand the nature of captivity from a wide angle lens. For many men it isn't a matter of 'one look you're hooked'. Many Christian men have been exposed to blurring cultural boundaries over the years with little impact on their sexual integrity. Yet others really struggle with remaining free from pornography's grasp. The level of an individual's captivity is mediated by several factors. Below is a simple model that frames the range of the captivity process.

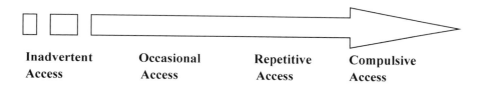

Inadvertent Access   **Occasional Access**   **Repetitive Access**   **Compulsive Access**

Imagine a graduated captivity process that spans from inadvertent looking to compulsive porn use. There is a qualitative distance between the two. *Inadvertent access* refers to the pornography exposure that people have that has little to do with their moral intent. A TV commercial, spam email and a misspelled word in an internet keyword search can yield these types of exposure. And while most inadvertent access can be minor, it shouldn't be underestimated; it can have tremendous impact in influencing a moral slide toward more illicit material. Recall that David's inadvertent peek off of his rooftop led to his sexual tryst with Bathsheba (2 Samuel 11).

Occasional access is a bit trickier to define. For example, if a person uses a computer as part of their job, exposure to illicit material can happen on an occasional basis. This can happen infrequently, but still happen if web filter software isn't installed on their computer. In this case it would also be inadvertent and accidental if there is no moral intent to surf porn. However, a person can also 'occasionally' and intentionally access pornographic material. They engage their will, and search for illicit content, or surf past questionable TV shows hoping to find a titillating nugget. They just do it on an infrequent basis.

Repetitive access refers to a person who is forming a habit of searching for and finding porn. Their access follows a pattern, and the pattern follows a repetitive process. A few years ago, one man I counselled indicated that he would wait until his wife went out on a particular night of the week. He would then use the home computer to search out pornography. Another would wait until people went home from the office after a day's work. Looking as if he was putting in longer hours than the rest, he would then surf the net for explicit content. People who repetitively access pornography follow general patterns of times, places and content that they search for. Some patterns may occur over periods of time, quarters or months of the year. Some patterns are more frequent, occurring over specific days, or times of days. The common feature is that they follow a repetitive pattern.

Compulsive access refers to a person's access of pornographic content in a way that is driven by strong feelings, compelling urges, and obsessive thinking. Porn use has become a drug of sorts and they are hooked. Explicit images, memories of things seen, or fantasies occupy mental and emotional space. Sexual impulses and urges drive the obsession for more. For these men, compulsive porn-search behavior is common. And consequences are disregarded.

Please understand that the model reflects broad categories on a general continuum. There are no clean criterion that can differentiate one person's use from another. Rather, a person (*being honest with themselves and others*) often has a good idea where they may fall on the continua. Where a person is situated on the continuum, and whether they are moving toward deeper captivity is mediated by several moderators.

Moderators

How quickly a person slides toward a greater level of captivity is largely influenced by several factors that mediate the process. These moderators refer to the level of secrecy that a person uses to hide their porn use, the quality and nature of time that they spend seeking and using porn, the amount of energy that they invest into their porn use, and their investment of money they spend in pursuit of their habit.

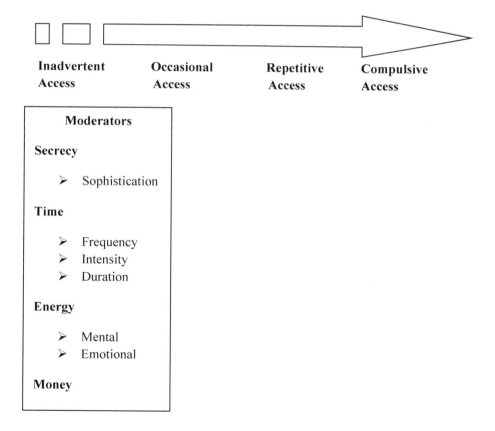

Inadvertent Access   Occasional Access   Repetitive Access   Compulsive Access

Moderators

Secrecy

➤ Sophistication

Time

➤ Frequency
➤ Intensity
➤ Duration

Energy

➤ Mental
➤ Emotional

Money

- **Secrecy**

Recall that secrecy is part of the UNSAFE model. This is important. Some secrets are acceptable, benign and don't carry a lot of weight. My children, for example are giddy when it comes to birthday presents for Daddy. They can barely hold back from telling me what they have made or bought for the big day. But they bite their little tongues and refrain from telling me because 'it's a secret'. This is not the case with pornography.

It has been my experience as a clinical counsellor that when a person has developed habitual or patterned access to illicit material, they bury it. They don't tell friends or significant others because of the guilt or shame that is attached. This seemingly small act has big consequences. Without exposing their secret to others, it festers and creates emotional turmoil. This turmoil, in many cases can later fuel more frequent or deeper access to pornography in the future. There is a saying in Alcoholics Anonymous - "your secrets make you sick". I tend to agree. Secrecy creates suffering, and the more a person distances themselves from others, the more toxic their process can become.

There is a second side to secrecy that I should mention. Some people that develop habitual access to pornography know that what they're doing is wrong, but they keep doing it anyway. Secrecy for these has the same elements of keeping it from others. However, the level of *sophistication* that a person goes to, to hide their porn use can also facilitate a greater slide on the continuum. Using other people's computer's, deleting a computer's history or temporary internet files, or searching several acceptable pages to repopulate the computer's internet search history after deleting the record, are all examples of sophistication.

In a similar way, driving to other parts of town to access a magazine store, where others may not know you, or watching late-night TV after the family has gone to bed are also examples or sophistication. As elements of secrecy they propel the captivity process.

- **Time**

Both the quantity and quality of time that a person spends searching for or accessing porn are important to the captivity process. For the person on the left side of the continuum, who inadvertently accesses illicit images, little time is spent engaging the material. However, the further toward the right an individual moves, time spent accessing and experiencing pornography plays a key role in their captivity.

Frequency refers to how often a person searches for and/or uses illicit content. It makes intuitive sense that the more frequently a person looks for and experiences porn, the greater a problem it might become. Frequency is a key factor in determining whether a person is sliding from occasional porn access toward repetitive access. Individuals who are forming a pattern of daily or weekly searches, are far more likely to form an attached relationship with porn, than those who accidentally or have occasional access with greater distances in time.

Intensity refers to how exciting the material is that one looks at. Given the euphoric nature of our God given sexual neurochemicals, the *hotter* the material is that a person accesses (based on their subjective preferences) the more addictive the material can become. A person will continue to seek that same level of experience in the future. However, given the nature of addictive tolerance, the person often needs to escalate their search in order to find the experience that they are now accustomed to. Looking for harder-core porn, new sex positions, or something more exotic then becomes the trend. In this case, a person continues to pursue more intense forms of pornography.

Duration refers to how long a person accesses pornography at the time that they are seeking it. A person seeking porn for five minutes, may be in a vastly different place on the continuum than a person who accesses it for five hours. When combined with intensity and frequency, duration can add fuel to the fire. The longer a person searches for preferred sexual content, the greater the likelihood of their success. And the more intense their experience, the more likely the person becomes captive to the sexualized medium.

- **Energy**

How much mental and emotional space a person gives to pornography is a key indicator of how important it is to them. Emotional energy refers to the types of emotions that are precursors to their porn use and those that follow. Mental energy is the amount of cognitive space that a person gives both to the approach of porn, and the aftermath of porn.

For example, in Bill's case (from the beginning of the chapter), awareness of his emotions, such as stress, became an important clue to when he was about to slip back into illicit material. In the build up toward porn use, frustration, stress, tension and other emotional clues served as indicators and potential warnings to an imminent fall. Further, significant emotional energy also went into the aftermath of his porn use. Guilt and shame were obvious consequences after viewing porn. In Bill's case, these emotions wouldn't dissipate for weeks, as he would continuously beat himself up for ignoring the Holy Spirit and proceeding willingly with the temptress. Emotions of depression, hopelessness and failure would nag him as well.

For Bill, mental energy was related to the content of his thought life pertaining to porn use. Leading up to a moral failure, Bill would spend much of his waking hours thinking about how and where to access pornography, or the content that he might search for when the time was right. Web sites that he had mentally bookmarked were gone over in his mind as he became preoccupied with the nature of porn that he'd seek out. In an almost obsessive way, Bill would become fixated on the target of porn.

Significant mental energy was also spent once he had consumed sexual images. Recalling and replaying the sexual content in his mind was automatic. Images would invade his memory without provocation. And dealing with the emotional toxicity of having accessed porn, he was preoccupied with how to maintain his secrecy. How to remain hidden, how to protect his image, and how to avoid public scrutiny consumed his time.

- **Money**

Despite a trend in the industry to give away pornography, this feature is only intended to hook an individual toward the medium. Money is the real objective. Once captive to the medium of pornography, the industry is betting that a person will inevitably spend their income on material that is more edgy and more sexually compelling.

Remember that pornography has an addictive element to it. Once hooked, a person will seek out stronger material in order to get the same emotional *'hit'* as they had in their earlier use. Often, the more compelling material will lead them to websites that cater to a person's idiosyncratic sexual tastes or fetishes. How frequently a person spends money, and the amount that they spend, provides clues to how captive a person really is.

TRAC

The individual's process toward captivity is assisted by a very simple micro-process. The TRAC model describes how an individual cycles from Trigger, Rumination, Acting-out, and

Consequences in the ever-tightening grip of porn use.

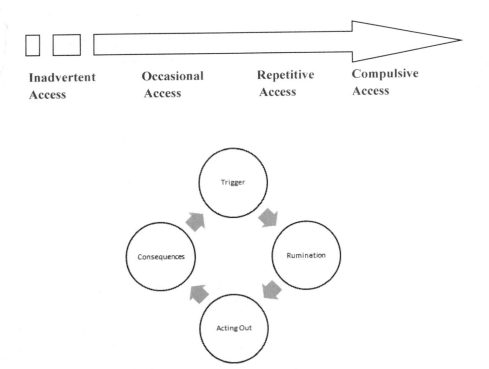

Inadvertent Access　　**Occasional Access**　　**Repetitive Access**　　**Compulsive Access**

Trigger

Rumination

Acting Out

Consequences

In Bill's case, the TRAC pattern was followed almost with surgical precision. In particular, he would spend mental and emotional energy, fixating on some topic of sexual interest. Triggered about its content or access-point, he would inevitably turn to how he might get it. Ruminating over the plan, he would think about what computer he might use, and how to cover his tracks once his covert operation was completed. Then, when the time was right, he would Act out and steal away moments with the seductress. Once finished, he would experience Consequences of guilt, shame, withdrawal from his community, and isolation. When paired with the moderating factors of increasing secrecy, time, energy and money, Bill became more captive to his ever expanding appetite for illicit material.

Captivity Criteria

The more captive a person becomes to pornographic media, the greater their preoccupation with it. Mental and emotional energy is spent seeking it out, and recovering from its use.

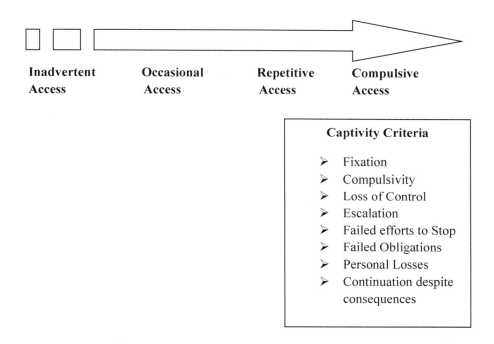

| Inadvertent Access | Occasional Access | Repetitive Access | Compulsive Access |

Captivity Criteria

➤ Fixation
➤ Compulsivity
➤ Loss of Control
➤ Escalation
➤ Failed efforts to Stop
➤ Failed Obligations
➤ Personal Losses
➤ Continuation despite consequences

Moreover, the captive person begins to compulsively seek out and use pornography. Despite trying to stop, they continue to pursue their sexual conquest. But yesterday's porn-high isn't enough. They need a greater level of sexual gratification, and seek deeper levels of illicit media. Their pursuit consumes so much energy that they lose track of time, so much so that they leave their obligations to work and relationships unfulfilled. The more they drop the ball, the greater the relational, social and occupational consequences. Yet despite these consequences and losses, they continue their search for a greater sexual conquest. In doing so, they withdraw from the relational resources that gave them life and support at one point in time. They become captive to the medium in search of feeling alive but instead reap death.

Tying it Together

Let's look again at the TRAC cycle at the center of the Captivity Process model. What makes pornography so captivating is its ability to influence the whole human system. In particular, the images that a man looks at obviously stimulate his visual field. But this is only part of it. Sensory, visual or auditory data then occupy his thoughts and influence his emotions. These also influence his physiology and neurochemical composition in such a way that the sexual medium becomes self-reinforcing.

Within the human sexual response cycle, the male body produces neurochemicals that heighten physiological sensations. During the Trigger and Rumination phases, a man may be thinking about sexualized images and how to obtain them. However, from a physiological perspective his testosterone levels increase in response to his sexual anticipation. Dopamine and norepinephrine levels focus his sexual attention, prime the body for sexual action and increase his sexual sensitivity. When at their peak, they produce a physiological state called myotonia in which a man is at heightened sexual arousal.

At this point most men act on their urges and impulses resulting in orgasm. At this point neurochemicals called endogenous opioids cause euphoric physiological sensations. And these mind-blowing sensations act like a super-drug.

Once these sensations reside, oxytocin and vasopressin are released in the body. These neurochemicals are known to bring feelings of satisfaction, closeness and bonding. In tandem, these ecstatic and calming emotions further anchor the man to the medium.

Within this process, sexual images become embedded in a man's memory with their pairing with strong physiological experiences, making them hard to erase from the man's mind.

Consequences such as guilt, shame and self-loathing often follow. Feeling poorly, most men begin a process of withdrawal from their personal relationships, church participation and accountability. Over time, they become more isolated. These emotions often act as catalysts for future episodes with the Temptress.

Pornography Captivity Process Screen

Instructions: Being completely honest with yourself, answer the following questions. Your time reference should be the past 6 months.

□ □ ⟹

Inadvertent Access	Occasional Access	Repetitive Access	Compulsive Access

Yes No   1.   I only see pornography accidentally and do not search it out.

Yes No   2.   I search out, or think about, pornographic images on an occasional basis.

Yes No   3.   I search, out or think about, pornographic images in a habitual, patterned or repetitive basis.

Yes No   4.   I compulsively search out and access pornography, or think excessively about pornographic images.

Secrecy

Yes No   5.   I hide my porn use from others.

Yes No   6.   I have lied about my porn use.

Yes No   7.   I have deleted the files or history from my computer or phone so I don't get caught.

Yes No   8.   Sometimes I rebuild an internet history on my computer to distract others from knowing what I've been looking at.

Yes No   9.   Sometimes I drive to different parts of the city to access porn and to avoid being seen.

Yes No   10.   Sometimes I surf the TV channels looking for explicit content when others aren't around.

Yes No   11. I make sure I leave no paper trail when I pay for pornography.

Time

Yes No   12. I find myself looking for pornography when I am online.

Yes No   13. I have been looking at stronger forms of pornography in the last six months.

Yes No   14. I have lost track of time when looking at pornography.

Yes No   15. I have not completed my obligations because of porn use.

Energy

Yes No   16. I think about how to access pornography all the time.

Yes No   17. I have tried to stop looking at pornography, but have been unable to stop.

Yes No   18. I become more frustrated and depressed when I have stopped using porn.

Yes No   19. I have experienced emotional, social or occupational consequences as a result of my porn use.

Yes No   20. I have been unable to stop my porn use, despite having experienced emotional, social or occupational consequences.

Yes No   21. I think about sex or pornography all the time.

Money

Yes No   22. I have spent money for sexually explicit material.

5

The Individual Nature of Captivity

A moments insight is sometimes worth a life's experience.
– Oliver Wendell Holmes

The tip of the Iceberg

"I'm the king of the world!"

I think everyone I know can identify these words, who said them, and the movie that they came from. If you are one of the few people who hasn't seen James Cameron's 1997 movie Titanic, the words come from Leonardo Dicaprio's character as he leans toward his future, arms raised in a celebration, wind in his face. A short time later he is one of the many victims of the ship's ill-fated maiden voyage.

The movie is of course, based loosely on the historical account of the RMS Titanic that hit an iceberg in 1912 and sank, killing 1500 people. Though most adults have a general idea about the history of the voyage and its outcome, few people know how it changed naval safety.

In its day, the Titanic was believed to be unsinkable; the product of the best engineering and technology that man could build. Upon its sinking the international community sought a coordinated system to prevent similar accidents. Within months, the US Navy began to monitor ice flows that could threaten passing ships. The following year, several maritime nations established the International Ice Patrol to monitor, among other things, the flows of ice that could compromise shipping lanes. In the decades that have followed, satellite and radar technologies have provided relevant data about the location and potential danger of icebergs.

The problem with icebergs lies within their nature. They are essentially huge blocks of ice that are mostly submerged beneath the surface of the ocean. In fact, regardless of its size or shape, only 1/9th of any iceberg is visible above the water line, the rest is underwater. And since no iceberg is the same consistency, the shape of what lies beneath the surface is unique to each iceberg. Passing ships only see the tip of the iceberg, not what lies beneath the surface. And therein lies the danger.

The iceberg serves as an excellent symbol for the nature of personal pornography use. For many men, what they allow others to see above the waterline is minimal. They manage their visibility of their porn use so that others may remain unaware of their personal choices. And the intricacies and unique factors of their porn use that lie beneath the surface can be devastating to the personal relationships and faith communities that they are part of.

For many men, thinking about the facets of their porn use is a foreign concept. They are content to simply keep the issue secret from others and struggle in silence. And yet, without an honest examination of the architecture of the nature of their porn use, they remain ignorant of its influence over their choices.

The Pornography Use Iceberg

The following diagram illustrates a working model that I use in the counselling and groups I facilitate. An overview of the model describes the components that are typical for people that struggle with captivity to explicit material.

Pornography Use Iceberg

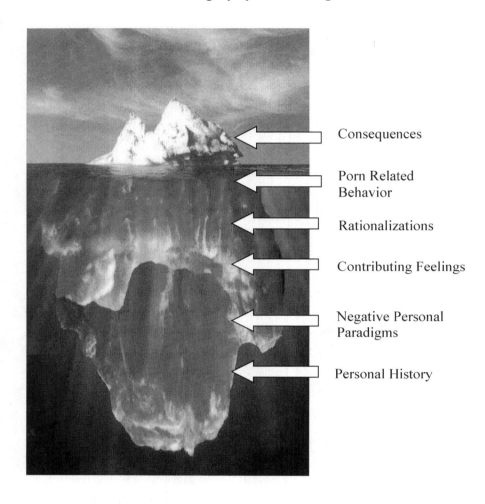

Consequences

Porn Related
Behavior

Rationalizations

Contributing Feelings

Negative Personal
Paradigms

Personal History

The questionnaires that follow are meant for an honest evaluation of your personal circumstances. I encourage you to work through them in complete honesty. Awareness is the first step toward freedom.

Consequences

Many men don't consider the costs of courting pornography. It is a consumer driven market that offers illicit content in any form in any location at any time. And most men access their preferred content in secret. Their reasoning is that if no one knows about it, no one can get hurt. This is where they are wrong.

Pornography is a consumer-driven industry, but it is those who view it that become consumed. Recall the indicators for pornography in Chapter 4. As a man immerses himself in repetitive or compulsive porn use, he begins to lose parts of himself. More mental space is occupied by illicit images or their sexualized conquest. More emotional energy is spent in planning or recovering from its use. And there is less concern for the social fallout of getting caught. There are always consequences.

Proverbs 7 talks about the death that men experience when they succumb to the temptress. It has been my clinical experience that men experience little deaths along the way to captivity. Parts of themselves submit to their growing appetite for porn and bits of themselves become eroded. Let me explain.

When most men start to purposefully seek out and experience pornography they consciously and willfully ignore the promptings of the Holy Spirit and exhortations from scripture to pursue Holiness. As their will stays engaged with the erotic medium, their will becomes weaker and less influential over their urges.

Eventually, their impulses drive their pursuit of illicit material. At the same time, their mind becomes consumed with the memories of what they have seen, or of unrealized fantasies, or new sites or resources that can be searched. As passion ignites into full flame, and captivity tightens its grip, the person's mental life (fantasy, sexual expectations, need for diversity and expansive content) becomes darker. People and other relationships can become sexualized.

Emotionally, porn use can briefly satisfy a man's desire, but it then craves more with a growing hunger. And there is a cost with their growing appetite. At an emotional level, most men move beyond their initial guilt and remorse as they sink deeper into the grip of captivity. Emotions of loneliness, depression and despair often follow along as the man loses hope in their ability to break free and shame overtakes them.

Physical consequences often accompany emotional and mental side effects of porn use. Loss of sleep, somatic complaints and stress headaches are just a few. Exhaustion from mental and emotional investment, or of managing a duplicitous lifestyle are common. Loss of interest in sex with their partner, or an escalating interest in diverse sexual experiences may be a further consequence that affect others.

There are spiritual consequences as well. As a man experiences pornography at deepening levels, he begins to callous. He is less sensitive to the Holy Spirit's promptings. Interest in spiritual things begins to wane. No longer is he interested in the needs of others, participation in his church or engagement in an active worship life. These things lose their importance. Rather, relational distance is often the route taken as it feels more comfortable and easier than facing others.

There are also social consequences to an individual's growing porn use. Initially, a man's porn use may feel innocuous as there are few who are affected. But as he builds his habit on deception and secrecy, he closes off parts of himself to others. Isolation, emotional distance and withdrawal cause others to wonder what is going on. When the habit is discovered, others are left with the feelings of anger, hurt and betrayal. In some relationships consequences may range from simple public exposure and humiliation, and in others, loss of friends, separation or divorce. When pornography use has occurred in public settings, such as work, an individual may face formal reprimands or termination.

Proverbs 7 is clear that there are death-like consequences for following the temptress. For their part, consequences sit right at the water line of the iceberg. For some, the consequences of their access of illicit material remain hidden from others, and at times from themselves. For others they bob into view for others to see. Regardless of their visibility they remain dangerous to all personal and social relationships that venture close enough to experience them. At any stage of captivity, becoming aware of the consequences of a person's access to explicit material is important. You can't change what you don't acknowledge.

On the following page is a consequence list. Review it and honestly indicate which consequences you may have experienced as a result of your porn use.

Consequence List

Spiritual

- ☐ Loss of interest in faith
- ☐ Loss of interest in worship
- ☐ Loss of interest in God
- ☐ Loss of interest in prayer
- ☐ Loss of interest in the Bible
- ☐ Loss of concern for others needs
- ☐ Less participation at church
- ☐ Less sensitivity to the Holy Spirit
- ☐ Pretending to be engaged

Emotional

- ☐ Increased loneliness
- ☐ Increased despair
- ☐ Greater sadness
- ☐ Increased anxiety
- ☐ Increased fear
- ☐ Loss of self esteem
- ☐ Increased shame
- ☐ Increased guilt
- ☐ Emotionally calloused
- ☐ Hopelessness
- ☐ Feeling alone
- ☐ Depression
- ☐ Suicidal thoughts
- ☐ Feelings of violence
- ☐ Greater anger

Mental

- ☐ Preoccupation with sex
- ☐ Intrusive sexual thoughts
- ☐ Sexualizing people
- ☐ Loss of self respect
- ☐ Inability to focus
- ☐ Distracted from responsibilities
- ☐ Increased sexual fantasy
- ☐ Need greater diversity of content

Willpower

- ☐ Loss of control over porn
- ☐ Compulsive porn use
- ☐ Frequent attempts to quit porn
- ☐ Decrease of will power
- ☐ Spend more time viewing
- ☐ Craving pornography
- ☐ Increased use at work or home

Physical

- ☐ Poor sleep
- ☐ Exhaustion
- ☐ Increase OR Loss of interest in sex
- ☐ Muscular tension
- ☐ Headaches
- ☐ Weight gain/ Weight loss

Social

- ☐ Distance and isolation
- ☐ Loss of trust
- ☐ Loss of emotional closeness
- ☐ Lying and deception
- ☐ Decreased sexual intimacy
- ☐ Increased demand for sexual variety
- ☐ Spousal feelings of betrayal
- ☐ Spousal anger & hurt
- ☐ Separation/ Divorce
- ☐ Distance from children
- ☐ Loss of time and energy
- ☐ Spouse feels compared to an unobtainable standard
- ☐ Loss of others' respect
- ☐ Loss of reputation
- ☐ Legal problems
- ☐ Police involvement
- ☐ Work-related probation
- ☐ Loss of job
- ☐ Loss of friendships

Porn Related Behavior

The temptress in Proverbs 7 whispers in the young man's ear. Her speech is punctuated with seductive imagery intended to incite his senses. She is sexually dressed to allure him, and has decorated her bed in colorful linen to seduce his sight. She has scented her room in aromatic spices to seduce his sense of smell. On top of that, she proposes ecstatic lovemaking for as long as he desires, seducing his imagination with fantasies of exotic variety. Whatever he can think of is there for his pleasure.

Pornography offers the same proposal to every person who is willing to entertain the pitch. Pornography use follows a pattern for most people who are occasionally, repetitively or compulsively accessing explicit material. In the same way that the young man in Proverbs 7 found the right street corner of the temptress, many men know where they can go to access their preferred contraband.

In particular, people tend to develop specific tastes for the type of sexual content that they prefer. These then follow patterns in a person's search for porn. An individual's preference for *people-types* such as body types, age groupings and skin color can serve as patterns for what a person looks at.

Similarly, the places that a person seeks pornography tend to follow a pattern. Specific locations such as magazine, movie or adult novelty stores may inform a person's unique behavioral pattern. Particular parts of town, or going to neighboring cities in order to avoid contact with someone that they know.

Sought out sexual content also tends to follow a pattern. Particular sex positions, fetishes, and sex acts may also be habitually sought out. And specific web sites, TV shows or rooms that are used to access pornography may also follow a pattern. Knowing a person's specific pattern can be helpful in helping them finding freedom.

On the following page is a porn related behavior list. Review it and honestly indicate which is a part of your porn use.

Porn Related Behavior Assessment

Most pornography use follows certain patterns. For example, a person may look at specific acts or people-types that reflect their preferences. Review the list below and identify patterns that you see in your own experience.

People- These reflect the typical preferences you have toward physical attributes of people in your porn use.

- ☐ Particular body types
- ☐ Muscular / Overweight
- ☐ Old / Young
- ☐ Male / Female
- ☐ Married / Single
- ☐ Vulnerable / Aggressive
- ☐ Large breast / small breast
- ☐ Particular ethnicity - Light skin / Darker skin: _____
- ☐ Past partners (identify) : _____
- ☐ Fantasy Partner (identify characteristics) : _____
- ☐ Will look at anything

Places - These reflect the typical preferences you have toward how you access your porn use.

- ☐ Magazine or movie stores
- ☐ Sex toy stores
- ☐ Specific locations - (areas of town, beaches, hotel rooms, bathrooms, vehicles, etc)
- ☐ Solitude / Privacy
- ☐ Specific TV shows or channels
- ☐ Specific rooms in your house / work (identify): _____
- ☐ No particular place - just wherever I can find it

Positions - These reflect the typical preferences you have toward the sexual activities in your porn use.

- ☐ Particular sex positions: _____

☐ Particular sex acts: _____

☐ Particular sex toys: _____

☐ Whatever is available: _____

Computer - These reflect the typical preferences you have toward the web-content of your porn use.

☐ Specific web sites (identify) : _____

☐ Home computer

☐ Work computer

☐ Daytime

☐ Night time

☐ Any time that I can get away with it

Rationalizations

For many men, the heat of seduction and sexual arousal of pornography imply they have stopped thinking rationally about what they are doing. What man in his right mind would willfully hurt his child, wife, friends or faith community? In the heat of lust and passion, these things stop being foremost in a person's thinking.

And yet for some, the search for pornography begins without the burning of non-rational passion. Some men think quite reasonably about why they should avoid pornography and yet pursue it anyways. Others provide self-justifications to exempt themselves from responsibility of their choices.

Rationalizations are the ideas and reasons that a person gives themselves, or others, to excuse their porn-related behavior. These can range from "No one will ever know." or "Just this one time..." to "She makes me so angry!" as means of self-justifying just a little peak at sexualized material. Excuses, denials, sense of entitlement and other justifications can make a use of pornography seem legitimate to the person searching at the time they are searching it out. And yet these rationalizations are not reasonable or logical when considered honestly or under the light of truth.

The patterns of rationalizations are unique to each person. And each provides an illegitimate form of permission for the porn-related behavior that a person uses. Exploring and knowing a person's specific pattern of rationalizations can be helpful in helping them finding freedom.

On the following page is a common rationalizations list. Review it and honestly indicate which you may have utilized in order to justify your porn use.

Common Rationalizations

By definition, rationalizations are statements that we tell ourselves to excuse our behaviors or feelings. In essence we explain our behavior in a rational or logical manner to avoid the true explanation. Look at the following list and identify which apply to you.

- ☐ It's not that big of a deal.
- ☐ I'll look for just a little while.
- ☐ I can deal with it on my own.
- ☐ If it weren't for _____, I wouldn't be in this spot.
- ☐ He / She makes me so mad.
- ☐ I have so much stress in my life.
- ☐ No one will know.
- ☐ I can look - I just can't touch.
- ☐ I just don't care.
- ☐ It really isn't hurting anyone.
- ☐ It runs in my family.
- ☐ It was just this one time.
- ☐ There's nothing wrong with it.
- ☐ I can't tell anyone about this.
- ☐ No one can tell me what I can or cannot look at.
- ☐ I can delete the computer files later.
- ☐ It'll never happen again.
- ☐ It makes me feel better.
- ☐ I can pray for forgiveness later.
- ☐ I can't put a blocker on my computer because _____.
- ☐ I don't have anyone I can be accountable with.
- ☐ I can overwrite the computer files so no one will know.
- ☐ They knew I had this problem before we got married.
- ☐ I don't have a problem.
- ☐ It's not my fault.
- ☐ Oh yeah - what about you?
- ☐ I deserve a little 'me' time.
- ☐ If she does it with me it is OK.
- ☐ Other: _____

Contributing Feelings

There is a feedback loop of sorts that influences the pornography use process. For men that access illicit material on an occasional, repetitive or compulsive level, emotions both precede and follow the TRAC cycle. And both can deepen the captivity process for the person who continually submits to their addiction.

Preceding the porn-related behavior, a man might feel anger or frustration toward his wife, or his circumstances. Things may not be going his way, work might be stressful or family relationships may be frustrating, and so his corresponding emotions weigh in on his rationalizations, making pornography seem like a legitimate action.

"If she was more attentive to me...", is really informed by the emotion of *anger* toward his wife.

"I just can't do this job anymore...." is really informed by the *stress* that he feels toward the mundane nature of his work.

"What's the point?" is informed by the *emptiness* of his current circumstances.

Becoming aware of typical moods or feelings that precede a porn use cycle is important in recognizing the signs of danger.

Emotions following pornography use are equally important to be aware of. Feelings such as shame, guilt, emptiness and depression can follow repetitive porn use. However, these can also serve to reinforce the desire and pursuit of illicit material in the future. In essence, a man's deep emotional pain may leave him feeling empty. Seeking something to medicate his emotions he in turn, seeks out pornography, and the cycle deepens. Becoming aware of a person's typical emotional state that contributes to their porn use can be helpful in helping them finding freedom.

On the following page is a Contributing Feeling list. Review it and honestly indicate which you may have experienced prior to, and as a result of your porn use.

Contributing Feelings List

Instructions: Think about the emotions that you feel when you are most likely to act in a self-medicating way. Identify which are common by placing a check mark in the appropriate box.

- ☐ Sad
- ☐ Rejected
- ☐ Angry
- ☐ Hurt
- ☐ Irritated
- ☐ Elated
- ☐ Fear
- ☐ Guilt
- ☐ Confused
- ☐ Weak
- ☐ Disgust
- ☐ Tired
- ☐ Stressed
- ☐ Resentful
- ☐ Oppressed
- ☐ Depressed
- ☐ Lonely
- ☐ Anxious
- ☐ Other:_____

Automatic Negative Paradigms & Personal History

For most people, emotions and moods can have their origins in the interactions with their everyday circumstances and relationships. Sun on their face or a hug from their child can buoy their feelings toward happiness or contentment. On the other hand, a broken water heater, an argument with their wife, or some shmuck cutting them off in traffic can summon frustration or anger. These emotions can be benign or, in themselves, provoke pornography use. For many others, emotions that are tied to habitual pornography use can be anchored to their personal histories or automatic negative paradigms that people hold about themselves. Let me explain.

Deep down, at the core of your being, what do you think about yourself? Are your thoughts positive, joyous and full? Are the first things that come to mind characteristics that make you unique and special? Do you see the things that make you fearfully and wonderfully made? Are you thankful for His handiwork? Or, do you mostly see your faults, failures and deficiencies? What populates your vision is important to your emotional health and has implications for porn use.

Paradigms are essentially the way we *see* our world. They are the interpretations and meanings of events and relationships around us. If I ask you to complete my sentence - "Police are...?, Politicians are...?, Women drivers are...?" - the words that you provide offer clues to what you believe. For some, the word police renders words like *necessary, good, or hero's*. For others it may yield *corrupt* or *abusive*. In the same way 'Politicians' may evoke words like *role models* or *civic duty*, while for others words like *liars* and *crooks*. Often, these paradigms are the mental architecture of how we make sense of our world.

Paradigms, whether positive or negative, are generally formed by many of our earlier experiences. Using the 'Women drivers are' scenario, many of us may have formed this idea in a way that stays fairly embedded; we believe that women have poor motor vehicle skills or spatial awareness. One process that leads to this kind of thinking is called *attribution*. For example, if a young man was learning to drive, and another car cut him off in traffic, he would most likely be startled and hastily respond. If he noted that it was a female who cut him off, he would have the seminal information required to build a paradigm regarding 'women drivers'. If in his discussion with others, the topic of women drivers was discussed in negative terms, he would further solidify his paradigm.

Now, here is the interesting part - the more anchored this paradigm becomes, the more it will reinforce itself. Should the young driver get cut off in traffic at another time, he will be more likely to pay attention to the gender of the driver. If it was a female, the event would further reinforce his beliefs as sort of an "I knew it! - they really are bad drivers!" kind of way. However, if it were a male that cut him off, he may not have the same reaction. He may attribute reasons for the other driver's poor driving; 'maybe he's late for work; maybe he has to pick up his kids...' In this way, the paradigm would filter and reinforce his thoughts about women drivers. The interesting thing about paradigms is that unless we question their validity, they can remain quite stable.

Here's where the concept of paradigms tie into the porn use iceberg. What's important to know is that we also have paradigms about ourselves. Core beliefs such as "I'm a failure", "I'm fake", "I don't measure up", and "I'm unlovable", can become part of our *self*-thought architecture, as a result of our personal histories. These personal paradigms, especially the negative ones, have tremendous power in driving our emotions and corresponding behaviours.

How these paradigms are formed is often the blend of several sources. Our families of origin communicate our worth at an early age. Their messages, whether spoken or implied, communicate the value and meaning of things like education, gender, and right and wrong. They also tell us the value of ourselves. For some, affirmation, affection and acknowledgement provide the backdrop for our identities. For others, rejection, criticism and devaluation were the norm. To paraphrase Donald Miller's book Blue Like Jazz, we learn that we are lovable or unlovable through people.

In the same way, victim stories are those negative narratives that we remember of the ways in which we were mistreated. Rejections in school, in academics or at sports can imply a message of devaluation to those who experience them. And our life choices can also provide evidence to our value though the span of our lives. Poor choices and regrets can also inform our negative personal narratives.

It has been my experience that many people who find themselves captive to pornography have negative personal paradigms that automatically pop into their heads intrusively. Though the beliefs "I'm a failure" or "I'm unlovable" can come from one of many sources, they tend to be a permanent fixture in one's thought life. And like Adam or Eve, the person hides these beliefs, afraid that someone else will find out.

Working upwards on the iceberg, often these negative paradigms, regardless of their origin, provoke strong emotions. These emotions eventually give way to rationalizations and the preferred sexualized behavior that is meant to medicate them.

"I'm a failure" provokes feelings of self-loathing. Self-loathing prompts an emotion of sadness and apathy. Strong feelings promote the rationalization that "It just doesn't matter" or "I don't really care". These thoughts permit the man to surf the internet or

TV stations until he finds his images of choice.

For the time that a person drinks deeply of the elixir of pornography, there can be a general sense of relief. But, this cure is brief at best, and really proves to be no cure at all. Like scratching a mosquito bite in summer, the relief is temporary, and proves to bring a stronger and more compelling itch after the scratching has stopped. A greater medicine is necessary to fix the personal struggle within one's core thoughts.

Knowing a person's automatic negative paradigms and where they came from can be personally insightful, and helpful in finding freedom. Review the exercises on the following pages and complete them with honesty.

Automatic Negative Paradigms

- ☐ I'm stupid
- ☐ I can't do math
- ☐ I can't read
- ☐ I can't speak
- ☐ I'm such an idiot
- ☐ I'm too sensitive
- ☐ I'm too emotional
- ☐ I'm weak
- ☐ I'm such a fake
- ☐ I'm a cry baby
- ☐ I'm a momma's boy
- ☐ I'm a drama queen
- ☐ I'm lazy
- ☐ What's the point
- ☐ I'm a procrastinator
- ☐ I'll never get it right
- ☐ God must hate me
- ☐ I am lost
- ☐ I am a waste of life
- ☐ I don't matter
- ☐ I am a failure
- ☐ I am evil
- ☐ I have no value
- ☐ I am dirty
- ☐ I am not capable
- ☐ I'm such a loser

- ☐ I'm too short
- ☐ I'm too tall
- ☐ I'm too thin
- ☐ I'm too fat
- ☐ I'm such a liar
- ☐ I'm too ugly
- ☐ I'm too old
- ☐ I'm too saggy
- ☐ I don't measure up
- ☐ I hate my _____ (nose, hair, eyes, ears, thighs, etc)
- ☐ I'm a terrible son
- ☐ I'm an awful grand child
- ☐ I'm a terrible brother
- ☐ I am an awful husband
- ☐ I am a terrible dad
- ☐ I'm a horrible friend
- ☐ I don't fit in
- ☐ I'm weird
- ☐ I'm not good enough
- ☐ No one likes me
- ☐ I am so empty
- ☐ I am unlovable
- ☐ I am uncoordinated
- ☐ I'm crazy

Personal History Questionnaire

Family

What messages did you learn about your value or lack of value from your family?

Regarding your past, what do you wish your parents would have done differently?

What messages did your family teach you about sex?

What family messages or experiences may still contribute to your porn use?

Victim Stories

What are some of the memories you have from your past that still cause you emotional pain?

How might these contribute to your porn use?

Choices

What are some of the choices you made in your past that still cause you emotional pain?

What are some of the choices that you made in your past that contribute to your porn use?

6

Steps to Freedom

The secret to happiness is freedom.
The secret to freedom is courage. - Thucydides

David

I've often wondered what David was thinking.

In the span of a few short verses, 2 Samuel 11 frames the captivity process of King David as he becomes intoxicated with the pursuit of Bathsheba. Think about it. In the cool of the evening, David is walking about his roof-top terrace. Out of the corner of his eye, he catches sight of a woman. Interested, he looks in her direction. Then it hits him, *she's nude*, taking a bath. But rather than turning his head and looking away, he fixes his gaze, he lingers and he is hooked.

Remember the Moderators of the Pornography Captivity Process, in particular Secrecy, Time and Energy. The bible doesn't tell us about the frequency of David's roof top viewing habits. But, we can make an educated guess about both the duration and intensity of the time he spent looking at Bathsheba. It is my belief that David had an immediate and intense rush of neurochemicals while looking at Bathsheba that caused him to remain fixed on the beauty of her female form. This wasn't a passing glance. David most likely rubbed his eyes, did a double take and strained for a clearer view. It was prolonged and intense. And, regardless of his personal assistant clarifying that this woman was the wife of Uriah and the daughter of Eliam, David continued his pursuit and conquest. He *had to* have her.

It is my opinion that Bathsheba had gotten inside of David's head.

The event and process didn't happen spontaneously. In the space of three verses, we go from *the rooftop look* to Bathsheba's declaration - "I'm pregnant". This jump implies that a lot of time had passed. I believe that in the space of time between the look and their sexual liaison, Bathsheba became an object of David's fixation. She occupied his head-space. She was the material of his sexual fantasy. And the more he fantasized and ruminated, the more space she occupied. He eventually acted out.

And immediately after Bathsheba confronted David with the news of her pregnancy, David set about to maintain the secrecy of their tryst. In increasing sophistication, David at first tried to create the illusion that the baby was Uriah's by summoning him from battle in hopes that he would sleep with his wife. The plan failed. David then set about to have Uriah killed, by sending him to the front lines where the fighting was most intense. Uriah died in battle. David then took Bathsheba as his own wife, no doubt trying to legitimize and hide the act. I'm sure that in David's mind he was successfully covering up his sin.

However, in 2 Samuel 12, the prophet Nathan speaks with the King. He tells David a story about a wealthy land owner that took a poor man's lamb and consumed it for his own benefit. David becomes incensed at what the wealthy man had done. And at that, Nathan tells David that the wealthy man in the story in actually David himself. At this, David repents and the Lord forgives him.

Psalm 32 is believed by many to be written by David about his relationship with Bathsheba. In it, he speaks of the emotional consequences of not only sinning against the Lord, but also of trying to hide it. Burying it, denying it or hoping it will just go away, doesn't ease the emotional backlash from surfing pornography. Secrecy is simply the mechanism that keeps us stuck.

Remember the concept of readiness in Chapter 1? Honesty with self is the first step to freedom. Honesty with self is the awareness of the consequences and unique patterns of porn use and the rationalizations we tell ourselves to justify our actions. Honesty allows us to look at the emotional content that contributes to our behaviour. These processes, and what they imply, can be difficult to face. Honesty about where these emotions originate, and their deeper meanings offer clues to our deeper longings.

But honesty with others is also an essential ingredient toward freedom. Secrecy insulates our actions from others' judgements and the condemnation of our guilt and shame. It shields us from other potential social consequences but it also holds us captive as our fear of exposure impairs our motivation to move. Honesty with others requires vulnerability, and this requires risk. Yet disclosure, within the safety of committed, caring and accountable relationships can bring about repentance and the keys to freedom.

The honesty that I am talking about has a softness to it. Remember that readiness remains open to others' influence, and allows for permission to try new things. It believes in change. In this case, honesty is informed by a person's desire for freedom. James 5:16 says *Make this your common practice: Confess your sins to each other and pray for each other so that you can live together whole and healed.* John 1:9 says *If we confess our sins, he is faithful and just and will forgive us our sins and purify us from all unrighteousness.*

Honesty pursues the truth, and the Truth will set you free.

Joseph

Genesis 39 is another interesting passage about lust.

The Bible says that Joseph was a well-built young man. This implies that he was good looking, young, and he had a well-defined physique. On top of his obvious physical attributes, he was intelligent. Over time, his business acumen and personal integrity became apparent. As a result, he was given more administrative responsibilities over Potiphar's business holdings. Genesis 39 says that God's favour blessed all that Joseph's hands touched in such a way that others were blessed through him. In our 21st Century culture, that could mean that he could grace the covers of either GQ or Forbes, or perhaps both. He had brains and brawn. To Potiphar's wife, he was a hottie.

Obviously, Potiphar's wife had noticed Joseph around her home. She had noticed his physical appeal. And over time, he became the object of her sexual desire. Her preoccupations, her sexual fantasies and eventually her aggressive pursuits were to have sex with this young man. But there was something unique about this young man; he was not interested in her advances. This, no doubt, drove her crazy. And after several attempts to seduce him, she realized that he was not simply playing hard to get. For Joseph, no meant no.

As the story played out, Potiphar's wife eventually cornered Joseph and demanded that he have sex with her. But for his part, he remained steadfast; he would not be seduced. As he ran for the door, she grabbed his cloak and later used it to frame Joseph for a crime he didn't commit.

Contrasting the stories of David and Joseph reveals useful content about the nature of Freedom. I believe that the downfall of David began with the head-room that he gave to Bathsheba. In a form of progressive escalation he looked at her naked form but did not avert his gaze. He inquired about her to others and he ignored the gentle nudge from the Father, that she was someone's daughter and someone's wife. Despite this, he pursued her sexually and then manipulated his circumstances to cover it up. David's mental and emotional world had become consumed.

In contrast, Joseph offered no head-space to the possibility of having sex with Potiphar's wife. Despite having looks, brains and power Joseph saw these as merely gifts given by God for him to steward. They didn't form his identity. And with these submitted to his God, the advances of Potiphar's wife held no appeal to him. And when he was cornered against the pressing advances of the temptress, he ran.

It is my opinion that for many men, the problem with pornography begins largely in their heads. It begins with a glance or a thought, takes on a life of its own and is maintained in secrecy. And the solution to the problem and continued freedom is in how they keep their head-space free from the allure of the temptation.

Remember, in today's culture, men have to go out of their way to avoid pornographic material. The question then becomes, what do they do with the images that may pop into their environment. Having a plan and resources to prevent the medium from taking up more cognitive and emotional room is essential for a man to remain free from its grip.

Evasive Maneuvers

A person doesn't have to be the captain of an ocean vessel to realize that when the ship is headed toward an iceberg, evasive maneuvers are necessary. In the same way that Joseph ran from the pursuit of Potiphar's wife, there are times that we need to take drastic action. Creating distance from illicit material and building skills for reducing its effect are paramount for staying out of its destructive power.

- **Intention**

Look back at Chapter 1. In particular, look at the questions that you answered at the bottom of the readiness questionnaire. To refresh your memory, the questionnaire surveyed how ready you were to look at the habits you may have formed regarding pornography. The first question asked you to look at some of the reasons you may have for why you may not be completely ready to change. The second question asked you to consider what it might take to become more ready.

The concept of intention asks a similar question. In particular, it asks *"What do you want to do regarding your pornography use"*. Regardless of whether you are a person who accessed illicit material inadvertently, occasionally, repetitively or compulsively, the question remains the same. For a man who is inadvertently exposed to porn, the response may be to merely learn skills to deal with the exposure. For others who repetitively or compulsively access explicit material, the response may be to become and remain free.

The most important part of intention is *internal*. It is recognizing the need for change and making the internal commitment to pursue change. It is doing the work to attend to the internal dynamics that provoke and enflame the lust towards pornography. It is doing the internal work to contend against these same temptations. And it is doing the internal work to tend and nurture oneself through the process of change.

The next most important part of intention is to make it *external*. Pursuing positive change means allowing others into the dialogue and struggle. It means choosing and then asking a *safe and trusted person or persons* into the struggle and telling them that you intend to change. This small step creates movement, and this movement begins the process of change. It also means that external resources are utilized in the process of pursuing freedom.

- **Attention**

If you have been honestly working through some of the worksheets provided in Chapters 1-4, you will have gained insight into some of the patterns that might exist regarding your porn use. Awareness of the particular preferences regarding sexual content, access points and specific behaviors removes the ignorance that a person has about their patterns.

Insight about one's rationalizations and corresponding moods and emotions forces a man to become aware of when he is more likely to act out with a sexualized medium. The process of insight about ones negative core beliefs and their origins opens the door for a man to deal with unresolved issues.

What's more, a man's insight provides an opportunity to find and believe his true identity, rather than the negative core beliefs that inform his current identity. And becoming aware of the deepest longings of his heart provides an opportunity to meet with the One who can satisfy them.

But let's be honest. A man can become aware that he typically acts out sexually when he is bored or depressed. He can know that he prefers to look at naked women behind the closed door of his home office when the rest of the family is in bed for the night. He can also be acutely aware of his preferred web sites or TV shows. And he can also know that he feels terrible about himself, confirming and reinforcing his core beliefs that he is a failure. And he can know that he is really trying to satisfy a deeper longing for spiritual intimacy, through an artificial and non-lasting tryst with the temptress. But awareness by itself won't create change.

When attending is linked to the intent to become free from the ambivalent dance with porn, there is a significant motive for change. For the man who is aware and committed, there is still work to be done, but the recipe for change is in place. The next step, contending, requires sustained motivation and action to be fruitful.

- **Contending**

What if I told you, that the way to beat your battle with pornography isn't in the valiant battle you wage with your will power, but rather through submission. That's right, submission, giving up, throwing in the towel. Don't get me wrong. I am not advocating the fatalism that says "I've lost, so I should just keep looking at porn". Rather, I am advocating a submission to the One who can set you free.

There is a saying in addiction support circles that loosely paraphrased indicates that a person recognizes that they are powerless to their behavior of choice and that only God can set them free. For the most part, the white knuckled, gritted teeth, will power fight against captivity is pointless. Countless numbers of people held captive to chemicals and behaviors have come to understand that their fighting harder against their preferred vise just makes them tired and frustrated. And many find themselves hopeless, depressed and desperate, when they realize that despite their promises and attempts to quit, they are still stuck.

The good news of the Gospel is that Jesus came to set the captives free. And it is God Himself who does the contending for us. Look at Mark Chapter 1. Jesus and his small band of disciples are touring the countryside. He enters the temple and begins to preach. And immediately demonic influences begin to manifest. At that moment, the Kingdom of God confronts the kingdom of darkness in a very real way. And the man who was captive to demonic forces was set free.

The process of freedom begins at the same point as the leper, prostitute and sick person in the Gospels. It is recognizing that we are in a place of brokenness, desperation and helplessness, and calling out to the One who has the power to set us free. It begins with confession to God, telling Him about all that we have been doing to break his heart and asking for His help. And it requires repentance, admitting to God that what we have been doing is wrong, and that we want to be free. 1 John 1:9 tells us that if we confess our sins, He is faithful to forgive us.

Again, most of us would agree that confession by itself isn't enough to keep a man free of his captivity to porn. Proverbs 26:11 tells us that in the same way a dog returns to its vomit, so a fool repeats his folly. Many men that I have counseled through the years have admitted to the beautiful feeling of freedom that they experienced upon confessing and repenting, only to fall back into the same old patterns of porn use.

To remain free, a person has to cultivate an ongoing sensitivity to the Holy Spirit *before* they succumb to the whispers of the temptress. And they have to maintain a short account with the Lord if they do slip back into the illicit medium. And in practical terms, they need to cooperate with God in building practical safeguards against their willful pursuit of pornography.

- **Transparency**

Looking at the lives of David and Joseph provides useful principles of contending to assist in keeping men free from the grasp of pornography. In particular, accountability, avoiding and averting are useful strategies to sidestep a moral failure.

One of the first places to practically begin while contending against personal porn use is to avoid the Temptress where she has normally met you. This means removing all of the points of access that are regularly used to gain illicit material. This may sound simple, but it really begins by opening up the dialogue of your personal habits with a safe and trusted other person. Remember that secrecy is a mechanism that holds people in their captivity. By opening the dialogue to another person, we bring our habits and tendencies into the light, weakening their grip on us.

James 5:18 tells us to make this our common practice: Confess your sins to each other and pray for each other so that you can live together whole and healed. The prayer of a person living right with God is something powerful to be reckoned with.

Remember the iceberg model (Chapter 4). With this in mind, discussing the particulars of our porn-related behaviour can be a starting point of confession. If another person knows how we characteristically access pornography and the general nature of what we go looking for and how we hide our porn use, the power of porn loses some of its grip. Forgiveness can be spoken over us for what we have done.

I am not advocating that a man tells the gritty sexual details of their particular porn-related conquests. Rather, by disclosing the *what, when and how* a person typically acts out with pornography, we (their accountability structure) can pray more specifically for their needs and know where their triggers are in the future. These can be entry points for transparent discussions in the future.

This form of transparency is important as it exposes the labyrinth of the intricacies that a person goes through to both obtain and hide their porn use. However, it also provides a means of escape. For example, when a man feels the pull of temptation, his trusted and safe person provides a proven ally against the enemy. Calling this person *before* a slip back into porn use can elicit prayer, resources and perspective and a potential way out.

- **Avoidance**

Contending against pornography and its allure also means planning practical steps to avoid and escape the medium. In the same way that Joseph sidestepped Potiphar's wife, we too can build in safeguards to stay clear of sexual temptation. A necessary and essential first step is to create a porn-free environment. This means destroying all forms of print-based or tangible material that serves as triggers for porn use. Remember the definition of pornography provided by Wendy Maltz. It is *"any sexually explicit material that is intended to be or is used as a sexual outlet."* This means that if it is a trigger for *you*, it has to go.

Practically, it means setting up an internet filter on your home computers. It means leaving the door open, with the computer monitor facing a public venue. It means not staying up after everyone has gone to bed for the night. And if you are triggered from a community location, you stop driving by the places of access.

Remember that most men fall after a period of being triggered and ruminating over what they will do. By removing access points we truncate the process before it gains momentum. Removing any paper-based, trigger-based products and computerized access points are essential for personal freedom.

As a side note, there are several really good internet porn filters on the market. Though installing them is essential, it is important to have a second person install them with their own private passwords. This step, though small, will prevent a captive person from disengaging them when temptation calls.

Revisiting the story of Joseph and Potiphar's wife for a moment reveals an interesting principle. That he resisted her advances is a testimony to his integrity and illustrates for us the need for contending against the pursuit of porn's temptation. However, I wonder what went through his mind when she finally chased him around the room grabbing his coat. I also wonder if he had been looking around the room for the nearest exit, or a route for a quick escape.

Planning prevention strategies is important to remaining free of repetitive porn use. So too is a plan for evasive maneuvers when the iceberg looms large. In particular, when the internal process of temptation becomes a compelling force, having an escape plan is essential for a man's survival.

Pre-thinking the antecedent triggers, emotions, and places that might trip you up in the future, what you will do to circumvent a slip, who you will call for support and what your plan of escape is a crucial step in contending for your freedom. Responding to the promptings of the Holy Spirit to stop is paramount to both surviving and thriving.

The following page has a worksheet to identify a 24/7 plan for evasive action in the face of strong temptation. In particular, it is designed to identify particular strategies a person can employ when the temptation of the seductress feels too strong to fight. Review it and answer some of the questions.

Evasive Maneuver List

Think about your typical or historical porn use. Note some of your common triggers and when and where you typically slip. What are some of the things you will do *to prevent* a slip back into porn?

What might be a trigger for you? Identify specifically in the space provided.

☐ A particular type of person (male, female, attractive, powerful, etc): _____

☐ A particular body type (muscular, ethnic, shapely, etc): _____

☐ A past partner: _____

☐ Porn, sex or movie stores: _____

☐ Particular areas of town: _____

☐ Specific TV shows: _____

☐ Specific TV Channels: _____

☐ Specific rooms (home, office, library, etc): _____

☐ Closing and locking computer room doors: _____

☐ Specific computer websites: _____

☐ Specific common feelings (see common feeling list): _____

☐ Specific thoughts or ruminations: _____

☐ Specific sounds: _____

☐ Specific smells: _____

☐ Specific physiological sensations : _____

When triggered, how can you escape?

☐ What can you do?
   o Leave the area
   o Avert my gaze
   o Distract myself

- Pray for God's help
- Practice relaxation
- Thought Stop
- Exercise
- Leave the door open to the public
- Face the computer / cell phone toward the public
- Turn off the computer / cell phone
- Pray for the other person
- Worship

☐ Where can you go that is a safe place?

_____

When triggered who will you call?

☐ _____

☐ What is their phone number ? _____

☐ What will you tell them? _____

- **Averting**

Quite simply, to avert means to turn away, to turn aside or to ward off. Within the context of pornography use it means to sidestep the advances of the Temptress when she approaches. Remember that within the framework of contending, avoiding means to build in safe guards to steer clear of the people, places and triggers that trip a person up. Following the symbolism of Proverbs 7, it means avoiding the street corners that the temptress is known to frequent. In contrast, averting has more to do with our actions when she is within our eyesight or earshot.

Remember also, that the medium of pornography is growing in diversity and volume, globally and on a daily basis. The issue is not whether a person will be exposed to explicit content, but rather what they do with it when they are exposed. Remember that David was simply strolling across his roof top when he caught a glimpse of Bathsheba. Using the Captivity Process model in Chapter 3, David's glance would count as an inadvertent access of illicit content. The fact that he lingered and gave cognitive room for his lust to grow caused him to remain in his sin. In practical terms averting means to find a way to break free of the growing power of temptation as it is happening.

The story of David in 2 Samuel 11 illustrates several concepts that are useful in averting the Seductress. Specifically, when a man is exposed to explicit content that he finds specifically tempting, literally averting his gaze limits the time that the images remain in front of him. And this small act is essential to breaking the grip of porn.

Think about it like this. How long does an average person look into the eyes of a stranger as they are walking down the street? For most people, it is about a second. And in that amount of time sufficient information is gained about their dress, demeanor and general mood. This is also true for inadvertent exposure to pornography. For many men one second is even too long to be exposed to sexual images. In this brief amount of time, these images can ignite their lustful hunger for more. And this, when they let loose, give birth to death (James 1:15). Learning the skill of literally *looking away* can stop the images from gaining power.

Following this line of thinking, David had to ask about the woman who was bathing. His attendant had to inform him who she was. This was Eliam's daughter, Uriah's wife, and she had a name. Recall that one aspect of pornography that is captivating to many men is the illusion of anonymity; not only for themselves, but also of the person being consumed. The image of their desire remains a nameless body or sex object, but has no identity.

Cultivating a practice of seeing the impersonal images as real people can help break the power of temptation. Knowing that this is someone's little girl (or boy), that they are precious, and that they too are the reason that Jesus ransomed his life provides a sobering reminder that their consumption is wrong. Cultivating the practice of praying for them, their circumstances or salvation can reinforce the practice of walking in personal freedom.

Another practice of averting relates to how a man is able to break free of the images that have been planted in his thought life. If he is able to look away and feel no further corresponding pull, he has gained a significant victory. If he can build a regular practice of averting his gaze he has learned a tool that might just help him remain free. However, once images, memories or fantasies have gained a foothold in his thought life, he is susceptible to become entangled once again. Learning the ability to avert one's thoughts as they are being tempted is a crucial habit to continued freedom. In the same way that Joseph would have said "Stop!" or "No!" to Potiphar's wife, men can learn and practice useful habits of Thought Stopping.

In practical terms Thought Stopping is a clinical intervention that can be used to derail a thought-action process before it gains too much momentum. In short, the process empowers the word "Stop" or "No", allowing either word to interrupt a thought as it is gaining strength. With practice the process can help a man remain free from intrusive thoughts holding him captive.

The process and practice of stopping ones thoughts is useful not only for images that slip past a computer filter, TV show or into a man's imagination. Recall the concept of attending for a moment. If a man cultivates the practice of becoming aware of his particular, triggers, rationalizations, emotions or negative personal paradigms, the practice of averting can stop these factors before they gain momentum. For example, a guy who recognizes that he is feeling agitated may recognize that he is feeling worthless and that these feelings and beliefs are normal precursors to a moral failure. By practicing the skill of Thought Stopping, he may successfully interrupt the porn-use cycle long enough to implement his evasive maneuver escape plan.

The following exercises are designed to help a man gain an understanding of both averting his gaze and thoughts. Though they may seem simplistic in their nature, they contain incredible value when mastered. Through practice and discipline, a man can use these simple strategies to regularly sidestep the allure of the Temptress.

Look away

Instructions: The following exercise is to build a habit of averting your gaze when you are exposed to something that you do not want to see.

- Choose a common point of reference in the room you are in. (ie. A clock, chair, book, etc)
- Look at the object.
- When you are ready, practise looking away from the object.
- Repeat the process. However in successive attempts, look away trying to be more deliberate and faster in looking away.
- Rehearsing this process will build the habit of quickly averting your gaze when questionable content inadvertently comes into view.

STOP

Instructions: The following strategy will take time, reflection and hard work.

- Note some of your stressful or intrusive thoughts. Select one that is mild in its intensity.

- Imagine the thought.

- Set a timer in short intervals (eg. 30 seconds). When the time sounds

  o Yell STOP! or NO!
  o For effect, have an elastic band on your wrist and snap it as the timer sounds and you yell 'STOP!' or 'NO!'.
  o Repeat this step a few times.

- Next, repeat the steps above, but this time whisper the word 'STOP!' or 'NO!' as you snap the band at the sound of the timer.

- Next, repeat the steps above, but this time imagine that you yell 'STOP!' or 'NO!' in your imagination.

- By rehearsing the process you will build the habit of stopping your intrusive thoughts.

- **Tending**

For every thorny problem there is a simple solution - and it's usually wrong. Fixing captivity to pornography requires more than just memorizing scripture or the occasional accountability session with the church pastor. The dilemma of captivity to pornography is more than a man's delight in illegitimate pleasure. It is complex and layered. It is more than looking at pictures. It is the slow callousing of the conscience against the Spirit of God. It highjacks our emotions, our reason, our intentions and leverages our brokenness for its own gain. It rewires our appetites and neural pathways to the illegitimate. And it leaves the ruined pieces of consequence on the floor. To borrow the imagery of Jeremiah 2, captivity has to do with the fractured cistern that we have dug for ourselves to fill a thirst that can only be satisfied in relationship with the One who loves us with a perfect and unconditional love.

Breaking the destructive pattern of habitual pornography use means following through with our intention to be free. It means attending to the thoughts, feelings and behaviors associated with the medium, and contending with the medium when it appears. However, finding and retaining our freedom also means nurturing our very souls. It means re-establishing a closeness and sensitivity to the Holy Spirit. It means finding and holding to who we really are, rather than the broken paradigms that our histories dictate; it means gaining control over our responses to the sexualized stimuli that vie for our attention on a daily basis.

- **Spiritual Disciplines**

There are practical things that a man can do to nurture his soul. When a man falls into a pattern of habitual or compulsive pornography use he typically begins to remove himself from activities that are remotely spiritual. Distance and isolation follow closely behind. Spiritual disciplines are a unique way that a man can begin to nurture himself toward greater freedom. Reading his bible, memorizing scripture and finding expressions of worship (*that he can relate to*) can be life-giving. Repentance, forgiveness and communion can renew his sensitivity to things of the Spirit. Fasting from technology, entertainment and even food can promote a deeper relationship with the Father. And prayer can become a more central and genuine element of his disciplines.

In recent years I worked with a young man who had struggled with both pornography use and sexual acting out with prostitutes. For years he had wrestled with depression, anxiety and self-loathing that were anchored to negative personal paradigms. As he eventually emerged from the grip of the Temptress he found several things to be of significant value. The first was that he joined a group of men that struggled with the exact sex-related issues that he did.

To his initial surprise, these were normal guys, and some he even recognized from church. Knowing that he was not alone was, in itself, life-giving. The fact that the group talked about their struggles and prayed for each other provided a measure of safety for this young man to begin to be honest with himself and others for the first time. With time, he was open to their suggestions and input, and was willing to try things that in the past he would not have believed to work.

A second activity that was significant in the young man's freedom was recommended at the men's group. Quite simply, it was prayer. To this point in his life the young man was familiar with prayer, but it was the kind of desperate prayer *("Oh God please help me…")* that would come either before or after a moral slip. The type of prayer that was recommended at the group was Centering Prayer; a type of prayer that is more peaceful, reflective and quiet, than other forms of fervent communication with God.

In short, Centering Prayer is a type of meditative, presence-oriented prayer. The value of this form of prayer was in quieting his mind, emotions and physiology while practicing being present with his creator. Though it was difficult at first (distractions and squirming), he eventually developed a rhythm of silence and prayer that he was accustomed to. In conversation with him, he indicated that this prayer process caused him to be more at peace and less tempted by his old triggers. An example of Centering Prayer is found at the end of the chapter.

- **Physiology**

Have you ever wondered what it must have been like for Adam to breathe his first breath in Genesis 2:7? Imagine - eyes blinking, gradually becoming aware of himself and surroundings, lungs expanding - *deeply* drinking in his first breath. Like waking up from the best sleep ever, his body would be completely relaxed. He would have had no busy-ness to command his attention. He would have had no day-planner, no agenda, no to-do list, and he would have had no muscular tension or stress headaches - just relaxation.

Research on stress and anxiety has found that people who are in a heightened state of arousal breathe differently than those who are relaxed. Tense people breathe in ways that are shallower and shorter in duration. They use their upper respiratory areas to breathe. Relaxed people breathe in ways that are longer and deeper, and breathe in a way that expands their stomachs. By learning to focus on the quality of their breath, a person can learn to take deeper breaths and practice being relaxed.

Recall that physiological arousal is often part of the captivity process, and in the same way, stress and tension can trigger emotions that are common within a person's porn-use cycle. Activities that bring about relaxation and peace are useful in the practice of tending one's soul. The practice of relaxation and deep breathing can lower tension and stress, while at the same time reducing the cognitive and emotional factors that set the stage for a moral failure. An example of a relaxed breathing exercise is found at the end of the chapter.

Although it may seem antithetical to the concept of relaxation, exercise is also a valuable discipline in the process of tending one's soul. Moderate exercise, whether walking the dog to running a half marathon, releases endorphins into the bloodstream. Beside the value of stress reduction and fitness, exercise can help with lifting human emotion. When paired with good nutrition, these benefits increase. Vitamins B, C, D and minerals zinc and selenium have also been linked to heightened positive emotion. And when these are further paired with a good sleep regimen a man's mood and energy resources can elevate. These resources help to nurture the human soul against the doldrums of flattened emotion that often precede a moral failure.

- **Meaningful Activity**

A central element of pornography-use is its pursuit of pleasure; a pleasure that is ultimately hollow and found wanting. Tending ones soul does not imply that a person deprives themselves of pleasure. Instead, it pursues activities that are ultimately full of meaning, and these activities can in due course be pleasurable. Let me explain.

A few years ago I taught an upper-level course on happiness to psychology students at a local university. As part of a two-part assignment I challenged students to plan and execute a perfect day. Many students slept in till noon, watched sports or movies all day and gorged themselves on their favorite foods. Their task was to pay attention to their corresponding emotions and how long they lasted. Almost everyone noted the same thing. The perfect day was pleasurable, but eventually felt empty. Feelings of happiness evaporated almost as quickly as they were experienced.

The second part of the assignment was to do something completely for someone else. Again, their task was to pay attention to their emotions and how long they lasted. Some students dropped sandwiches off to the inner city's poor and homeless, and some paid for strangers coffees at a drive through. One student, upon seeing an elderly woman with a broken down motor scooter, pushed her (groceries and all) a half mile to her home. At the assignments conclusion, everyone noted the same thing - to their surprise. Emotions of happiness and satisfaction were elevated, however everyone reported that these were far more than those of their 'perfect day'. What was more, these emotions lasted for weeks as students recalled their contribution to complete strangers. The exercise illustrated the value of purposeful activity.

Within the context of pornography use, meaningful activity can relate to content that is connected to their particular style and level of interaction with the medium. Reading books on pornography addiction, attending meetings regarding sexual purity or engaging in bible studies related to wholeness can be just a few. In the same way, activities like personal journaling, participating in inner-healing prayer ministry or engaging in professional counselling can help in the process of healing and nurturing the soul.

Moreover, activities that correspond to the meaningful contribution of others can be useful in the process of healing. Whereas therapeutic activities are essential, they tend to continue a person's focus on themselves. Activities that are other-centered take the focus off of oneself and place it on the needs of others. And these activities in themselves can nurture the soul. Taking food to the less fortunate, volunteering for civic or church-related needs, and going on short-term (even city specific) missions projects can push a man beyond his self-absorbed sexual compulsion to begin to see the needs of others. And these activities can promote personal freedom. To paraphrase the American theologian

Fredrick Buechner, the place God will meet you is the place where the world's deep needs and our deep gladness coincide.

Adams Breath

Then the LORD God formed the man from the dust of the ground. He breathed the breath of life into the man's nostrils, and the man became a living person. Genesis 2:7.

Instructions: The following strategy is designed to promote relaxation through deep breathing and will require refection and practice.

- Get into a comfortable posture and relax your body.

- Concentrate on your breathing for a few moments. Is it full? Is it shallow? Are you breathing from your chest or from your stomach?

- As you do the next step, try to concentrate only on your breathing.

- If you can, try to silence the rest of your 'mental noise', in order for you to focus on your breath.

- Now, take one breath in. Make it deep and hold it for three seconds and exhale slowly (for another count of three).

- Once you are finished, take another breath in and hold it for three seconds, exhaling slowly for a 'three count'.

- Once you are finished, take one more breath in and hold it for three seconds exhaling again slowly for a 'three count'.

- Continue to breathe slowly on your own, but gently become aware. Slowly become aware of:

  o The sensation of air passing through your nostrils.

  o The rise and fall of your chest.

  o The pressure of your clothing against your skin.

  o The sensation of air against your skin.

  o The pressure of furniture against your body.

  o The rise and fall of your stomach.

- Now that you have finished, become aware of your body - do you feel different? More relaxed?

Centering Prayer

But when you pray, go to your inner room, close the door and pray to your Father in secret. And your Father, who sees in secret, will repay you. Matthew 6.6

Instructions: Centering prayer is not a technique. It is a form of reflective and meditative prayer intended to deepen our relationship with God.

- Select a sacred-word as the symbol of your intention to consent to God's presence.

  o Ask the Holy Spirit to inspire you with a word that is suitable for you. Choose one that has significant meaning for you - (ie. Jesus, Abba, Father, Freedom, Love, Peace, Mercy, Trust, Thank-you, etc).

- Find a quiet location and sit comfortably with your eyes closed.

  o Slowly begin to breathe in a slow and rhythmic pace.
  o Take one breath in. Make it deep and hold it for three seconds and exhale slowly (for another count of three).
  o Do this several times as it feels normal.
  o Silently introduce your sacred-word as you become aware of God's presence within you.
  o Focus on your breath and the word that you have selected.
  o Become aware of the presence of God within you.
  o On your inhale, focus on God's presence.
  o On your exhale, repeat your sacred-word as a prayer to the Father.
  o When distracted, gently pull your attention back toward the presence of God.
  o Try to participate in this form of prayer for 20 minutes, twice a day.
    ▹ If this is difficult, begin with shorter periods of time (5 or 10 minutes) in order to build your capacity for prayer.
  o When you are finished praying, remain sitting in silence with your eyes open for a few minutes.

Psalm 46 Breath

"Be still and know that I am God" Psalm 46

<u>Instructions</u>. The following strategy is designed to promote relaxation through deep breathing and will require refection and practice.

- Find a quiet location and sit comfortably with your eyes closed.

  o Slowly begin to breathe in a slow and rhythmic pace.
  o Take one breath in. Make it deep and hold it for three seconds and exhale slowly (for another count of three).
  o Do this several times as it feels normal.
  o Ask the Holy Spirit to help you quiet your mind and body.

- As you sit quietly, repeat the section of Psalm 46 as follows:

  o Be still and Know that I am God
  o Be still and know that I Am...
  o Be still and know...
  o Be Still

- Continue to breathe slowly and rhythmically

- Repeat the section of Psalm 46 as follows several more times:

  o Be still and Know that I am God
  o Be still and know that I am...
  o Be still and know...
  o Be Still...

Why Quit?

It is a terrible thing to see, but have no vision. - Helen Keller

No really... Why quit?

The first conversation is always interesting. I am talking about the first time that a man (or couple) sit in front of me to discuss the specific matters that they are bringing to the table. Sometimes we enter the topic slowly after some pleasantries, and other times the people are clamoring to get on with it. Eventually I get around to asking the question.

So, why do you want to stop pornography use?

Their answer to the question is very important because it inevitably reveals the architecture of the value structure that lies beneath their answer. Let me explain. At one level, their answer tells me a bit about their level or readiness discussed in Chapter 1. If a man hedges his information with half-truths or excuses he is demonstrating a measure of deceit, hoping to circumvent a deep and honest level of discussion. Normally, revisiting a conversation about readiness is important to clarify the ingredients for positive change. Honesty, openness, permission and expectation of positive outcomes are all essential parts of constructive movement.

Yet at another level, the answer to the question exposes whether the motive for change is internal or external. In particular, their answer reveals whether they own their captivity and process of change or whether they are motivated by external factors.

Have-to & Ought-to

I recall two young men that I saw several years ago. During the session with one of the men he informed me that he had been okay with his use of explicit material and hadn't believed that it was a problem for his marriage. His wife had discovered his habit, and strongly disagreed. She threatened that if he didn't see a counselor, that she would leave the relationship. During our conversation, it became apparent that the young man was really in counselling to avoid the consequences that had been threatened by his wife.

Sitting before me on another occasion was the second young man. During the session we began the discussion about why he was seeing a professional counselor. While there was genuine contrition in his voice, he was seeking counseling because he got caught using pornography while at work. The fallout from the event was that he was fired from the company and the residual effects were wearing on his marriage and church relationships. During our conversations he was ambivalent about change but reasoned that he *should* remove the habit from his life because he was a Christian and the Bible said that he should abstain from sexual immorality.

In both cases each man had a genuine and personal reason to quit their porn-use. But in both cases, each man was motivated by external factors. They reasoned that they either *had to* or *ought to* remove their habit.

The motivation and purpose for change for both Have-to and Ought-to is external to the person. It is not the man himself that desperately wants change, but rather an external motivator that is pushing the agenda of change. The threat of consequence, a personal ultimatum, or quasi-moral reasoning provides the content for his motivation. But these are external rather than essential and internal. They are more related to a response to other parties than an internal desire for change on the part of the man in question.

While these motives may be useful to provide purposeful movement at the beginning, they are not sustaining. The man who submits to them may for a time live within their confines. But eventually, he will fight against them, or become bitter against the people he sees holding him there. He'll live with one foot in the process of change, but also remain with one foot out of it. What's needed for sustained freedom is for the motive for change to be more essential and internal.

Want-to & Get-to

Whereas Have-to and Ought-to are external in nature, Want-to and Get-to are internal. A man that genuinely wants to be free is motivated by a deep desire for personal freedom. He surveys the cost of his selfish choices toward the Temptress and has a genuine sense of remorse and regret, and these in turn inform his desire for repentance. He wants to be free.

Let's be clear, the lepers and prostitutes did not come to Jesus because they *had to*. Nor did they reason that they really *ought-to* catch him while his healing ministry was in town. Rather, they pressed through the cultural and religious social consequences because they deeply *wanted-to* experience freedom. They were desperate and knew that He was the only One that could set them free.

Where want-to is a motivation to find freedom that comes from an internal desire, *get-to* is motivated by privilege and identity. This is the motivation behind Paul's endurance of beatings, shipwrecks and hardship. It is the motivation behind Jesus' scorning the cross, for the joy set ahead of him. Their inspiration was based on the reality of Heaven, rooted in their hearts, set before them. When asked the "why quit?" question, have-to and ought-to answer "because of the consequences" or "because it's a good idea" or "because the Bible says to". In contrast, Get-to answers "because He loves me".

I remember as a young man, hearing a pastor tell a simple story that illustrates the concept of get-to. Once there was a wealthy land owner who had many attendants. Every morning, the land owner ate breakfast and was served by a beautiful servant-girl. The landowner was pleased with the faithful care given by the young woman. Over time he eventually became enamored with her. As his love grew for her, he asked her to be his wife and the two were married.

The morning after their wedding celebration the landowner sat in the kitchen and pondered their relationship. Just then the young woman entered the room. The landowner asked her if, because they were now married, she was still going to make him breakfast or whether another servant would perform the task. To his great joy, she responded. "Before, I served you because I had to. Now I will serve you because I want to"

The concept of getting-to stop using explicit media is rooted in the nature of the relationship that we have with Jesus. Its use will always be a cheap counterfeit used to quench our deep thirst. And only a deep, rich and intimate relationship with Him will break the chains of captivity that hold us in our spiritual poverty. Knowing how much He loves us, and who we are as sons of God are essential to sustained freedom.

Peter - the Rock

One of my favorite passages in the New Testament is in Matthew 16. Jesus had been travelling the countryside preaching the good news, healing the sick and releasing those who were held captive or oppressed. And as a result He had acquired quite a following. The desperate wanted to be near Him in order to be free. The onlookers wanted to see what would happen next. And the religious elite wanted to criticize His work.

One evening Jesus was sitting with His friends and He asked them "Who do people say that I am?" Without missing a step, the disciples responded that the locals were saying He was like John the Baptist, or Elijah, Jeremiah, or one of the other prophets. Jesus followed with another question "And how about you? Who do you say I am?"

Peter was the first to respond. "You are the Christ, the Messiah, the son of the living God". And Jesus responded, not to the many, but to Peter himself.

"God bless you, Simon, son of Jonah! You didn't get that answer out of books or from teachers. My Father in heaven, God himself, let you in on this secret of who I really am. And now I'm going to tell you who you are, really are. You are Peter, a rock. This is the rock on which I will put together my church, a church so expansive with energy that not even the gates of hell will be able to keep it out. And that's not all. You will have complete and free access to God's kingdom, keys to open any and every door: no more barriers between heaven and earth, earth and heaven. A yes on earth is yes in heaven. A no on earth is no in heaven."

Now here is my question - How do you think Peter heard those words?

I mean, c'mon - this was heady stuff. These were significant words of praise and endorsement. These words were prophetic, and validating, and significant. They contained elements of his role in the future of God's kingdom, and they were powerful. On one hand I could almost see him looking at his peers with a sense of pride and surprise, as if to say "Did you hear what He said about me? I'm important!"

What I think is more realistic however, is that Peter most likely looked over his shoulder as if to say "Who...me?" or "Are you sure you have the right guy?" This was Peter the fisherman, not a prized profession of the religious elites of his day. This was the same Peter who, only a few lines later, was being publicly rebuked as Satan by the very Jesus who had praised him. This was the Peter who fell asleep in the garden when Jesus needed him to pray; who cut off Malchus's ear in protest to Jesus' arrest; and who denied even knowing Jesus on three separate times that same evening. This is the same Peter who Paul had to rebuke (in the book of Galatians) for showing preferential treatment to those of Jewish decent. These were not your typical *rock-like* behaviors.

Peter knew who he was, and most likely looked at himself and wondered, how will I ever get from here (fisherman) to there (rock-like)? The good news for Peter, and us, is that Jesus looks at us not through the lens of the present of who we are, but through the length and span of time and who He is making us to be. He is not limited by spiritual shortsightedness. He knows who we are, shortcomings and all. And He knows the events that will shape and form us twenty years from now. And He who began a good work in us, will carry it on to completion (Phil 1:6). The good news is that God has a panoramic view of your life and plans to prosper you as you fully seek after Him (Jeremiah 29). Peter simply needed to be faithful in pressing into and loving Jesus, and investing his life. He needed to be obedient in following the One who loved him most (John 21).

Recall the concept of Automatic Negative Paradigms in Chapter 4 for a moment. It is my belief that a lot of men walk around with negative conceptions about themselves that are rooted in their personal history. They believe that the title "Failure" or "Unlovable" or "Unforgivable" are their true identity, because they made poor choices at one point in their life, or because someone once made a pronouncement over them. And these beliefs remain 'true', limiting them from the freedom that they could walk in, if they could experience the intimacy of Son-ship.

Identity

Let's revisit the question that Jesus asked Peter - "Who do you say that I am?"

I believe that when Peter answered, he was answering for himself, not the collective opinion of his peers. He was saying to Jesus, "You are the Son of God". You are *my* Christ and *my* Messiah. And Jesus, upon recognizing Peter's confession says to him - now that you know who I really am, I am going to tell you who you really are. And it is this Jesus that defines our true identity.

I don't believe that when Jesus was asking about people's opinions of Him, that He was having an identity crisis. I don't think He was seeking personal validation, or performing an opinion poll to see if He had a good reputation.

There is a great little section of scripture in John 13 that you'll miss if you don't look for it. Jesus was in the upper room, and was soon to face His own execution. And in preparation, He is getting ready to wash His disciples' feet. And in this section the Bible says parenthetically that Jesus knew that the Father had put all things under His power, and that He had come from God and was returning to God. This was Jesus, who in John 1 was at the very beginning of all things, in face to face communion with God. This was Jesus who, when emerging from His baptism heard the words of his Father say, *"You are my son, I love you! I am pleased with you! You bring me Joy!"* These words are a picture of security, identity and purpose.

It is my belief that one of the keys to personal freedom from the temptress is anchored in *our* identity as a child of the Father. It doesn't come from merely hearing the words "I love you". It comes from the deep penetration of those words into one's soul. To paraphrase Ephesians 3, it comes from the deep rooting and establishing of our identity as *loved-ones*. It comes from profound abiding with the One who is love. It comes from the dwelling in His presence that we may be filled to the measure of all the fullness of God, understanding how big it really is.

Ideas have consequences.

Believe that you are a failure, justifying your belief with the evidence of history, and your behaviors will fall in line. Medicating your beliefs and emotions with the salve of pornography will provide temporary relief, and in the end captivity and death for your soul.

Believe that you are a deeply-loved child of God, who is ransomed, who is forgiven and whom He loves to spend time with, and the temptress will have less influence over your choices. Your pursuit of righteous and purity will be a privilege in serving the one who loves you with an everlasting love. This is the essence of *'get-to'*.

On the following page is an exercise designed to help with rightly defining your identity. Spend some time to earnestly work through it.

Biblical Truth Exercise

Instructions: Look at the following list of biblical truths. Select the ones that have the most personal meaning to you; the ones that resonate in your soul.

- ☐ I am faithful (Ephesians 1:1)
- ☐ I am God's deeply loved child (John 1:12)
- ☐ I have been justified (Romans 5:1)
- ☐ I am Jesus' friend (John 15:15)
- ☐ I belong to Him (1 Corinthians 6:20)
- ☐ I am a member of Christ's Body (1 Corinthians 12:27)
- ☐ I am assured all things work together for good (Romans 8:28)
- ☐ I have been established, anointed and sealed by God (2 Corinthians 1:21-22)
- ☐ I am confident that the Father will perfect the work He has begun in me (Philippians 1:6)
- ☐ I am a citizen of heaven (Philippians 3:20)
- ☐ I am hidden with Christ in God (Colossians 3:3)
- ☐ I have not been given a spirit of fear, but of power, love and self-discipline (2 Timothy 1:7)
- ☐ I am born of God and the evil one cannot touch me (1 John 5:18)
- ☐ I am blessed (Ephesians 1:3)
- ☐ I am chosen (Ephesians 1:4, 11)
- ☐ I am holy and blameless (Ephesians 1:4)
- ☐ I am adopted as God's child (Ephesians 1:5)
- ☐ I am in Him (Ephesians 1:7; 1 Corinthians 1:30)
- ☐ I am redeemed (Ephesians 1:8)
- ☐ I am forgiven (Ephesians 1:8; Colossians 1:14)
- ☐ I have purpose (Ephesians 1:9 & 3:11)
- ☐ I have hope (Ephesians 1:12)
- ☐ I am included (Ephesians 1:13)
- ☐ I am a saint (Ephesians 1:18)
- ☐ I am God's co-worker (2 Corinthians 6:1)
- ☐ I am a minister of reconciliation (2 Corinthians 5:17-20)

- [ ] I am alive with Christ (Ephesians 2:5)
- [ ] I am God's workmanship (Ephesians 2:10)
- [ ] I have peace (Ephesians 2:14)
- [ ] I am secure (Ephesians 2:20)
- [ ] I am a holy temple (Ephesians 2:21; 1 Corinthians 6:19)
- [ ] God's power works through me (Ephesians 3:7)
- [ ] I can approach God with freedom and confidence (Ephesians 3:12)
- [ ] I am completed by God (Ephesians 3:19)
- [ ] I can bring glory to God (Ephesians 3:21)
- [ ] I have been called (Ephesians 4:1; 2 Timothy 1:9)
- [ ] I can be certain of God's truths (Ephesians 4:17)
- [ ] I can have a new attitude and a new lifestyle (Ephesians 4:21-32)
- [ ] I can forgive others (Ephesians 4:32)
- [ ] I can give thanks for everything (Ephesians 5:20)
- [ ] I am strong (Ephesians 6:10)
- [ ] I am dead to sin (Romans 1:12)
- [ ] I am not alone (Hebrews 13:5)
- [ ] I am growing (Colossians 2:7)
- [ ] I am promised eternal life (John 6:47)
- [ ] I am victorious (I John 5:4)
- [ ] I am chosen and dearly loved (Colossians 3:12)
- [ ] I am blameless (I Corinthians 1:8)
- [ ] I am set free (Romans 8:2; John 8:32)
- [ ] I am safe (I John 5:18)
- [ ] I am no longer condemned (Romans 8:1, 2)
- [ ] I am not helpless (Philippians 4:13)
- [ ] I am a new creation (2 Corinthians 5:17)

Instructions: Reflect back on the Automatic Negative Paradigms that you had selected on page 63. Now look back at the scripture selections from page 100. Write down the Automatic Negative Personal Paradigm in the space provided on the left side of the page. Using your selections from the exercise on page 100, write down the biblical truth that contends with the paradigm. Reflect on the truth over the coming weeks.

Example:

Automatic Negative   Biblical Truth

I am a reject   I am no longer condemned
                                   (Romans 8:1-2)

I am unforgiveable   I am forgiven
                                   (Ephesians 1:8; Colossians 1:14)

I am worthless   I am God's deeply loved child
                                   (John 1:12)

I am evil   I am a deeply loved child of God
                                   (John 1:12)

I am lost   I am found (2 Corinthians 6:1)

I am weak   I am strong (Ephesians 6:10)

_____   _____

_____   _____

_____   _____

_____   _____

_____   _____

_____   _____

8

Epilogue

I have set before you life and death... Now choose life...Deut. 30:19

It's an interesting piece of naval history that Shackleton and his men *all* made it safely home following their failed expedition on the Endurance. That fact sets it apart from other naval disasters of its day. What is more surprising to me however, is that Shackleton and his men all planned a return to the Antarctic a few short years later.

For their part, the Endurance crew had arrived back in England as the First World War waged on. Shackleton enlisted and took various posts that supported his country's war efforts. But as the conflict came to an end and civilian life eventually became ordinary, Shackleton's thoughts once again turned toward the Antarctic. And despite some of the men not receiving payment for their last adventure with their captain, almost all signed up to pursue his vision. His new ship was re-christened the "Quest".

In an ironic twist of circumstances Shackleton would never make it back to the heart of the Antarctic. He died of a heart attack shortly after arriving at the island of South Georgia in January 1922. He was buried on the island where a memorial still stands.

What I find interesting as a footnote to his adventure is that Shackleton would want to return to the Antarctic at all. For that matter, I find it shocking that any of the men would re-enlist for a second round in one of the most inhospitable environments on the planet. They had just spent years of their lives fighting for their very survival in this place and had just returned home to the warmth and safety of their families. And now they were returning to the belly of the earth where their trials first began.

I often wonder what it would take to compel such men to re-enlist. Was it the thrill of the quest? Was it duty or obligation? Was it for the challenge? Was it for posterity?

I suppose on one hand, joining one's mates would have provided a significant point of connection. These men had been through one of the most trying ordeals of their lives and survived it together. And they had endured *together*. Their severe and common adversity had built an uncommon bond. Every man had had to play his part. Their very survival depended on it. And in the blast-furnace of this trial the bonds of fraternity, friendship and support had been forged.

The story of Shackleton and his men is one of adventure, danger, despair, hope, endurance and freedom. And its story applies to men's connection to pornography. It begins quite simply with the feeling of adventure that one has when they are called and seduced by the Temptress. And before long they realize the danger that they are in when titillation turns to captivity. And for many men, their failed attempts to break free from pornography's grip leads to a resigned sense of despair that they will be forever captive. Shame and secrecy keep them isolated in their solitary prison.

But it is in the ranks of their brothers that men can find hope. It is with hard work, support and the encouragement of others that repentance can turn them away from their sin toward the one who can set and keep them free.

It is my sincere hope, that if you are stuck in the grip of captivity to pornography that you seek the help of others. Remaining in secrecy and shame merely maintain a cycle of isolation and death. Choosing to bring your struggle into the light of day, in the community of faithful believers can help to deliver you into freedom. The choice is yours.

THE JOURNEY

One day you finally knew

What you had to do, and began,

though the voices around you

kept shouting

their bad advice –

though the whole house

began to tremble

and you felt the old tug

at your ankles.

"Mend my life!"

each voice cried.

But you didn't stop.

You knew what you needed to do,

though the wind pried

with its stiff fingers

at the very foundations,

though their melancholy

was terrible.

It was already late

enough, and a wild night,

and the road full of fallen

branches and stones.

But little by little,

as you left their voices behind,

the stars began to burn

through the sheets of clouds,

and there was a new voice

which you slowly

recognized as your own,

that kept you company

as you strode deeper and deeper

into the world,

determined to do

the only thing you could do –

determined to save

the only life that you could save.

Mary Oliver

Notes:

Notes:

120

Made in the USA
Charleston, SC
29 December 2016